HOOSIER HANDBOOK ®

Stories, Stats and Stuff About IU Basketball

By Pete DiPrimio and Rick Notter

ISBN 1-880652-51-X

Printed in the United States of America by
Mennonite Press, Inc.

First Printing October 1995

PHOTO CREDITS Photographs on pages 1 and 50
were provided by Dave Beasley. Photographs on
pages 12, 13, 14, 15, 17, 19, 20, 21, 22, 23, 24, 25,
27, 29, 30, 31, 32, 33, 34, 35, 38, 39, 40, 41, 45
(top), 46 (bottom), 59, 60, 68, 69, 70, 72, 73, 75,
76, 77, 79, 81, 84 (both), 86, 89, 90, 91 (both), 92,
94 (both), 95, 96, 98, 99, 100, 101, 103, 104
(both), 105, 106, 108, 109, 110, 111, 113, 114,
115, 117 (top), 118, 119, 120, 121, 122, 123, 124,
125, 126, 127, 128, 129, 130, 131, 132, 133, 134,
135, 136, 137 (both), 138, 139, 140, 141, 142, 143,
145, 147, 148, 149, 150 and 151 were provided by
the Indiana University Athletic Department
Archives. Photographs on pages 7, 8, 9, 11, 45
(bottom), 46 (top), 47, 48, 49, 51, 53, 54, 55, 56
and 82 are from the files of Inside Indiana.

ACKNOWLEDGMENTS

To compile a book on the history of Indiana basket-ball is no easy task and there are a number of people we would like to thank. First, thanks to Bill Handy, Kim Redeker and their colleagues at Midwest Sports Publications who helped make this project possible. Also to Jeff Pulaski, the artist who designed the cover and the book, for making this a visually-pleasing project.

From the research end, this book would not have been possible without the help of the Indiana University Media Relations Department and the Indiana University Library, whose records allowed us to learn almost every-thing we ever wanted to know about IU basketball. The bulk of the photographs in this book come from the Media Relations Department Files and include some rarely-seen photos of the early years at Indiana. Sports Information Director Kit Klingelhoffer and assistant SIDs Gregg Elkin and John Decker were all very helpful and supportive during the compilation of this book. We also want to thank the dozens of basketball managers over the years who took the time to keep excellent records and newspaper clippings from nearly every season.

We also must take the time to thank those journalists from years gone by whose work had an impact in piecing together the history of Indiana basketball. Writers from the Indiana Daily Student, Indianapolis News, Bloomington World, Indianapolis Star and Bloomington Herald-Telephone, whose work often was not credited, provided the stories that, in some cases, are the only record of events surrounding IU basketball.

Most importantly, we would like to thank the staff of Inside Indiana: Alan McDonald, Paul Jourdan and Mary Notter. They all picked up the slack in the office when Pete DiPrimio and Rick Notter were working on this book over the summer.

Finally, we would like to thank all those IU fans who have subscribed to Inside Indiana and/or those who buy this book. Their love for Indiana basketball is the driving force behind each issue of our paper. Hopefully this book will help that love continue to grow.

To my family. Without their support, this project never would have been finished.
– Pete

For my father, Dr. Richard Notter, whom I admire more than he will ever know. And to my family – Mary, Katie and Rich – my great-est joys in life.
– Rick

INTRODUCTION

From its humble beginnings around the turn of the century, Indiana basketball has grown into a phenomenon rarely seen on any college campus, or in any state in the nation. Indiana is second only to UCLA in NCAA titles and is the only school to win national championships in four different decades. IU's fan support has few peers in all of college basketball.

While Indiana has a rich tradition in basketball, dating all the way back to the enormous success enjoyed under Coach Everett Dean, we decided to begin this book with the most recent coach – Bob Knight. He will be remembered as the greatest coach in IU history, and perhaps the greatest college coach ever.

Coach Knight plays a significant role in the history of Hoosier Hoops, and therefore also has a significant section of the book devoted to him. But there was IU basketball before Coach Knight, so there is plenty to learn about Hoosier Hoops after the Knight chapter. Read on to see how basketball was first formed at Indiana University, how the arenas have changed over the years, how the Hoosiers claimed their first victory ever, first win over Purdue, first Big Ten Title, and first NCAA Championship – more than 30 years before Bob Knight arrived on campus.

Indiana basketball is more than Bob Knight, more than Assembly Hall, more than the NCAA Championships. It is a way of life that grew out of a state's love, make that hysteria, for a simple game involving a ball and a basket.

As it has been said many times: "Basketball was invented in Massachusetts, but perfected in Indiana."

Read on to learn how that state's best college team perfected the game in its own way.

TABLE OF CONTENTS

The Knight Way

Bob Knight.

Rumor suggests Bob Knight has mellowed. Don't believe it. The man who, in the summer of 1995, reprimanded the NCAA committee that reprimanded him, the man who still takes angry walks home from airports despite near-double-digit mileage, shows no loss of intensity.

Forget the gray hair and expanded waistline. A quarter-century in the national spotlight finds Knight as vigorous as ever, coaching with the energy of a man half his years.

Perhaps Knight has found the fountain of youth in controversy's epicenter. How else do you explain the continuing sideline histrionics, the never-ending incidents, the tirades ferocious enough to stop a charging bull at 10 paces, all while winning at a Hall-of-Fame pace?

Logic tells you Knight won't coach forever, that eventually even he will wear down and retire to full-time fishing and hunting.

But then, logic holds nothing on Knight.

He is a combustible combination of integrity, intimidation, charisma, profanity, competitiveness, intelligence, impatience, compassion and loyalty. No one demands more. No one inflames more people while doing it.

The public persona has raged in newsprint and on TV for a generation: the coach screaming, grabbing, kicking, swearing. Doing it his way, by God.

Such instant images can bury the substance. His players graduate. His program is clean. And yes, he does have a heart.

Knight helped Ryan White when the youth was dying of AIDS. He was there for Landon Turner after a car accident left the player paralyzed. He's raised hundreds of thousands of dollars for the university and charities; he's donated time and money in countless ways.

Of course, Knight wins. Heading into the 1995-96 season, he had 659 career victories, three NCAA championships, an NIT title, Pan American and Olympic gold medals, and a record 11 Big Ten crowns. The Hoosiers had been to 10 straight NCAA Tournaments, 19 in his 24 years.

Knight has won four national coach-of-the-year awards. The Big Ten has honored him six times. He is a member of the Basketball Hall of Fame.

Occasionally, there are the public relation disasters of his own creation. His Don Quixote tendency to fight windmills – what Knight has called battling "the rabbits" instead of "the elephants" – often clashes with politically correct sensibilities.

The result is controversy, much of it surrounding his treatment of players. But Knight is more than the bully image. He has to be. If not, either nobody would play for him, or his players would have rebelled years ago. Either way, his teams wouldn't win.

"People don't understand that nobody cares for us as players and people more than Coach Knight does," Damon Bailey said. "He's around us year-round. He'll do anything for us."

Yes, there are the volatile moments, the unorthodox methods, not just of sight and sound, but of mind. Players long ago began calling this BK Theater, concentrating on the message rather than the delivery.

"When Coach yells at me, I think it makes me better," Calbert Cheaney once said. "You go out and try to do something right. That's your way of getting back at him. Every time he yells at me, I say, 'Take that... or that.' "

It's been that way since Knight started coaching. He demands much – and expects much. He wants players so mentally tough that they cannot – will not – be beaten. He uses his voice as a bludgeon when it serves his purpose.

And there is purpose to his apparent madness.

A more reserved Bob Knight talks with IU and NBA player Greg Graham.

Knight tries emphatically to get his point across to former Hoosier Steve Hart during the 1994-95 season.

The philosophy is to be the best you can be. The method is hard work, discipline and determination. Those seeking shortcuts need not apply.

At times, this is basketball program as boot camp. Only the strong survive – and succeed. The championship banners that sway almost magically in Assembly Hall are testimony to that. So is the 95-per-cent-plus graduation rate.

"In order to understand the things that have happened here over the years, you have to understand the word 'effort,'" Knight has said. "If we get the right kind of effort, that kid will play. If we don't, he won't.

"Effort is multidimensional. It involves mental and physical exertion. It also involves paying attention to what has to be done. I don't think that's asking too much."

And so Knight goes his own way, sometimes with the tide, often against it. Mellowing remains for others.

THE KNIGHT WAY Knight has only one rule – do it his way or you're gone. He coaches hard; he fishes hard; he hunts hard. He wants the hardest working players, not necessarily the best.

"What people don't understand about me," he once told the Los Angeles Times, "is that I've always coached as if I were still at West Point."

CONSTANT DEMANDS Knight pushes his players to the limit, which doesn't always make him popular.

Isiah Thomas said there were times when, if he'd had a gun, he would have shot Knight. There were also times, he said, when he wanted to hug Knight and tell him he loved him.

In a 1993 story in Profiles Magazine, former Illinois player Marcus Liberty said, "I used to watch him scream at his kids and just shake my head and be grateful I didn't have to go through that. Looking back at the way those Indiana players turned out and the way they talk about the guy, if I had to do it over, I would have gone to Indiana, instead."

ON THE IMPORTANCE OF BEING LIKED When once asked if he wanted to be liked, Knight recalled a comment by Joe Lapchick, the former St.

Coach Knight showed his emotional side when embracing his son, Patrick, following Pat's final home game at Indiana. Knight later said Pat was his "all-time favorite Indiana player."

John's coach.

"His approach was, from a coaching standpoint, if you make decisions on whether or not you're liked, then you're not going to coach very well. That's the way I've coached from that day on."

Knight once told a group of reporters that "The thing you guys have to understand is that I don't agree with everything I do. I do some things to get things done that I don't particularly like."

In a 1994 interview with NBC's Bob Costas, Knight said he sometimes regrets his harshness.

"I can't tell you the number of times I've gone home and said, 'God, I wish I hadn't gotten on that kid like that.' I wish I didn't think I had to get on him...."

ON HIS CRITICS "I've often said this to some of the sanctimonious, self-righteous critics that I have," Knight told Costas. "I would hope when Judgment Day comes, they don't have to appear before St. Peter's table with me and only one space available for both of us and the judgment being made on which of us has done the most for his fellow man. I have no doubt St. Peter will turn to me and say, 'Robert, pass through the gate.' "

THE SOFT SIDE One night, before the 1986-87 season, Knight noticed a large group of students lined up outside the Assembly Hall ticket office. They planned to camp out all night to get season tickets the next morning. Knight sent them 40 pizzas in appreciation for their interest.

Knight has given his shoe contract money to the IU Foundation for basketball related expenses and academic purposes. He has raised more than $5 million for the library. During the Hoosiers' 1985 world tour, he took Indiana Athletic Director Ralph Floyd, 81-year-old Henry Iba and 87-year-old Everett Dean because all three had just lost their wives and Knight didn't want them to be alone.

RETIREMENT TALK Knight, whose contract extends into the next century, is often asked when he will retire. In 1988, he said he couldn't see himself coaching past age 57. He was then 47. Knight will turn 57 on Oct. 25, 1997.

LONELY WARRIOR "There are lots of times when I feel like I'm a lone ship on a stormy sea and I don't have any sail," Knight told Sports Illustrated.

COACHING MOTIVATION Knight told the Chicago Tribune in 1991 that "If I'm going to coach a team, I want it to look as if it's been coached. I want it to look as if it knows what it's doing. I want it to play well. I want players to feel that having played basketball was a very important thing to them. So I work to get that done, and when I can't get that done, I won't coach anymore."

Knight earlier told Joe Falls in the Detroit News that his one big remaining ambition was to "Put together a team better than the 1975-76 team."

HOW TO BE REMEMBERED

"When I'm done coaching and I leave Indiana University, whether they've liked me or disliked me, there are going to be two things people are going to be able to say about me," Knight once told the Indianapolis Star. "Number One is that I was honest and Number Two is that I kissed no man's ass. I can't mold myself to what other people want me to be."

Knight also added this quote from Abraham Lincoln: "If at the end of this administration, I have only one friend left, and that friend resides deep inside me, then I will be satisfied with what I accomplished."

The thrill of victory can often bring out the positive emotions in Bob Knight.

TIME FOR A CHANGE

The 30-year-old Knight – the first Hoosier coach since Leslie Mann was hired in 1923 who hadn't played at IU – was a surprise choice in the spring of 1971. North Carolina State's Norm Sloan, California's Jim Padgett and Clemson's Tates Locke had been the most prominent names mentioned.

But the four-man search committee was unanimous. In six years at Army, during a turbulent era when the military was least attractive to high school prospects, Knight's record was 102-50. He led the Cadets to four National Invitation Tournament appearances, finishing third once and fourth twice.

Knight accomplished this despite never having a player taller than 6-6 (West Point's maximum height allowance). The key was a man-to-man defense that finished among the nation's top three five consecutive seasons and was No. 1 three times. His teams never allowed more than a 58.5-point average.

This was uncharted territory for Indiana, where offense had often been priority No. 1, and sometimes No. 2 and No. 3. In 1963, the Hoosiers scored 101 points against Illinois and lost by three. The next year, they scored 103 against Michigan State and lost by four.

School officials wanted a change.

"Defense was a concern," IU Professor Edwin Cady, a member of the search committee, told the Indianapolis Star at the time. "But, in my own mind, it was more a combination of youth and an extraordinary record for a man his age."

Discipline was another factor. A student of the writings and philosophies of such military men as Gen. George Patton and Sun Tzu, Knight had no problem asserting his authority.

Bob Knight, with team captain Doug Clevenger and a statue of General Patton, as pictured on the back cover of the Army basketball media guide in 1970.

"Say this is discipline," Knight told a group of reporters, raising a hand to chest level. "This is military discipline (raising his hand to his chin). And this is my discipline (putting his hand above head)."

A LITTLE BACKGROUND Knight was a reserve on the outstanding Ohio State teams of the early 1960s. Mostly, it was because of such talented teammates as John Havlicek and Jerry Lucas. Partly, said Buckeyes Coach Fred Taylor, it was because Knight "couldn't guard Marilyn Monroe in a phone booth." Unhappy on the bench, Knight often talked of quitting, although talk never became reality.

Knight considered law school before becoming a high school assistant basketball coach at Cuyahoga Falls, Ohio. While there, he set records for broken clip boards that reportedly still stand.

After a year, he became an assistant to Tates Locke at Army. Two years later, at age 24, he was the head coach. Time Magazine later wrote "PFC Knight earned $89 a month and all the cadets he could eat."

While at Army, Knight was offered jobs at Wisconsin, Minnesota and Northwestern, but turned them down because he believed he wasn't ready.

When the Indiana position opened, Knight felt he was. Hoosier officials agreed.

Coach Bob Knight in 1971.

"Of all the men we interviewed, it was our unanimous opinion that he has the leadership to carry on the tradition of winning basketball at IU," said Athletic Director Bill Orwig.

Added Cady: "There wasn't any doubt in my mind. He was my choice from the very beginning."

School officials downplayed concerns Knight's deliberate, methodical offensive style – his Army teams never averaged more than 68.5 points – would turn off Indiana fans accustomed to high-octane attacks.

"I'm confident he's smart enough to play the type of ball he has the talent for. He won't do away with great offensive basketball," said Bill Armstrong, then president of the IU Foundation.

Added George McGinnis: "It sounds like he prefers pattern ball. I'm not knocking it, but I'm not really that kind of player. If I feel I can beat a man one-on-one, I'll do it. But whatever's good for IU is good for me. I'm sure it'll turn out for the best."

MCGINNIS LEAVES That best didn't include McGinnis. Shortly after Knight's hiring, he turned pro.

McGinnis told Inside Indiana Knight wasn't a factor. He said his father's death in a construction accident had created money concerns.

"After my Dad died, our family was left in a financial void," McGinnis said. "I left (school) because it was an opportunity for me to help my mother. It was a situation that was out of my control. It was something I had to do."

McGinnis signed with the Indiana Pacers, then a powerhouse in the now-defunct American Basketball Association. He played four years there, becoming a two-time All-Star and winning the league's most valuable player award. He led the Pacers to two straight ABA titles.

McGinnis later signed with the NBA's Philadelphia 76ers. He retired after the 1981-82 season.

McGinnis, whose 29.9 scoring average in 1971 remains the highest in IU history, said while turning pro was the right decision, he's wondered what would have happened had he stayed.

"A lot of guys on the team joked with me afterward that I never could have lasted. I'm sure it would have been hard to play for Coach Knight, but I could have. I know I'd have been a better player in the pros if I had stayed those two seasons."

THE INTRODUCTION

Knight was introduced on March 31, 1971. It was a busy first day. After a lengthy press conference in Indianapolis, he rushed to visit high school standouts John Garrett of Peru, Ind., and Pete Trgovich of East Chicago Washington.

While neither became Hoosiers (Garrett went to Purdue; Trgovich wound up at UCLA. Knight also was turned down by Jerry Nichols for Purdue, Indiana Mr. Basketball Mike Flynn for Kentucky and Junior Bridgeman for Louisville before landing his first recruit,

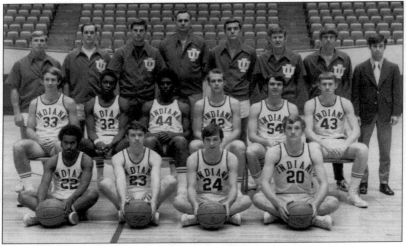

The Hoosiers of 1971-72, the first team coached by Bob Knight.

Steve Green), the tone was set.

"The foundation has to come from the freshmen we are going to have," Knight said. "We want to make sure we are going to have an excellent foundation."

Other priorities included picking a staff, getting to know the current players, studying personnel and developing a preseason conditioning program.

Knight said he wanted a team built along the lines of the 1960-62 Ohio State squads.

"My only hope is to make Indiana the best possible basketball program we can," he said. "I have some ideas on what I would like to see it become, but I'd rather keep those to myself."

FIERY WAYS Even then, Knight was known for his temper and competitiveness. His Army nickname was Bobby T for the number of technical fouls he received. He had once splintered a wooden chair during a heated discussion with a referee.

Tates Locke recounted this story from their Army days. It seems one year the Cadets were playing Washington State. By halftime, Locke and Knight each had two technicals. In the locker room, Locke couldn't find Knight. Finally, Knight walked in, head down.

"Come on, Bobby," said Locke. "We have to work out how we're going to handle the second-half tip."

"Don't worry about it," said Knight. "We're going to start with them shooting a foul. I just got another technical."

THE DEBUT

Knight quickly broke with IU tradition. At the first practice, a large group of alumni gathered as they always had. Knight threw them out.

What they missed was an intensity Hoosier players had never seen before.

"The thing most of us were not used to was how hard we worked and how long we worked in practice," Steve Downing told Inside Indiana. "The intensity was great. Previously, we were a little more relaxed and joked around. This was strictly a business approach to practice. We were always going, always moving."

As the season opener against Ball State approached, IU officials continued to emphasize Knight wouldn't abandon the fast break.

"In Bob Knight, Indiana has, in my judgment and that of the most knowledgeable observers in the game, one of the upcoming great coaches of the sport," Orwig wrote in a preseason brochure.

"…. I'm confident Indiana fans will like Bob Knight and the basketball his squads will play. Bob has a tremendous national reputation for building great defensive teams, stemming from his No. 1 and high-ranking defensive teams at West Point. The fact that he emphasizes defense and disciplined play does not take away the cherished fast break of Hoosier fans. Bob likes and appreciates the running game, just as when he played it with those great Ohio State teams of 1960-62.

"Defense can be exciting, too, as anyone who watched Steve Downing blocking shots last year can attest. I believe it will add a new dimension to Hoosier basketball with no loss to the fast and furious action that Indiana fans hold dear."

Knight also addressed the issue in the brochure.

"I like my teams to play what has been called a controlled fast break. In other words, I believe in disciplined basketball and I'm concerned with character, not characters. I think it suffices to say that no matter what you're doing on the floor – whether it's playing defense or on a fast-break – it has to be disciplined.

"…I stress good defense because I feel it is the basis of winning in all sports. I present it as a real challenge to the squad. That's why I prefer man-to-man to a zone. Everything is done on an individual basis, where we fully expect each man to do

Steve Downing was one of the first stars, and first All-Big Ten player of the Knight era. He continues his association with IU as an associate athletic director.

his job....

"Emphasis on discipline and defense does not mean we won't fast break. When I was at Ohio State, we liked to run when the opportunity presented itself. We'll fit our system to the players and the better defense we play, the more fast-break chances we'll get."

At first, IU fans didn't appreciate Knight's approach. In Lou Watson's last year, the Hoosiers averaged 90.8 points and allowed 86.1. Under Knight the next season, it was 73.6 and 67.1. The records were nearly identical: 17-7 for Watson, 17-8 for Knight.

"...He comes in and says we are going to pass the ball around and worse ... we were going to play defense," Downing said. "Fans weren't used to it."

As victories mounted, defensive appreciation grew.

"The emphasis he put on defense and the time we spent on defense in practice was probably the most amazing thing to me about Coach Knight," said Downing. "The players accepted it because Coach Knight sold us on the fact that if we did A, B and C and played the game the way he thought it should be played, we could win. And that was the bottom line."

REBOUND RECORD In the 84-77 defeat of Ball State, in the first game ever at Assembly Hall, Downing grabbed 26 rebounds. That remains the arena record.

Downing also burned Kentucky for 47 points and 25 rebounds. His 17.5 scoring average was second on the team to Joby Wright's 19.9.

The Hoosiers, once ranked as high as fifth in the nation, went 9-5 in the Big Ten. A five-game losing streak knocked them out of the conference title hunt, but they won nine of their last 10 regular-season games to earn an NIT bid. Princeton beat them in the first round, 68-60.

THE 1972-73 SEASON

Knight debuted the motion offense, which featured screens, crisp passing and precise cutting. Gone were the set plays that had marked his earlier teams.

The payoff was immediate. IU won its first five games and 14 of its first 16. The Hoosiers' 11-3 Big Ten record gave them their first outright conference championship since 1958.

Sophomores Steve Green and John Laskowski, who had dominated the freshman team the year before, made major contributions. So did freshmen guards Quinn Buckner and Jim Crews. Buckner, also a standout football player, became an instant starter despite practicing just three days before the season opener against Harvard.

NCAA TOURNAMENT Led by Downing, Indiana's first Big Ten Most Valuable Player since Archie Dees in 1958, the Hoosiers took aim at UCLA's invincibility.

Tournament victories over Marquette and Kentucky set up a Final Four showdown with the top-ranked Bruins.

UCLA took a big second-half lead before IU rallied within striking distance in the closing minutes. Then came the play that still haunts

Hoosier fans. Bruins center Bill Walton, with four fouls, got the ball, drove for the basket and collided with Downing. Officials whistled Downing.

"That was my fourth foul," said Downing. "Had it gone against Walton – and it should have been a charge – it would have been his fifth.

"A couple of minutes later, I actually did foul and was gone from the game."

Without Downing, who finished with 26 points, Indiana lost momentum and the game, 70-59. The Hoosiers bounced back to beat Providence 97-79 for third place while UCLA won the championship.

"It's kind of ironic," Downing said. "I see Walton all the time. The IU fans still ride him about that foul. He told me, 'I'm so tired of these Indiana people getting on me about that foul. You tell them I didn't referee that game.'"

ALL-AMERICAN Downing averaged 20.1 points and won All-American honors. He became the Boston Celtics' No. 1 pick and played on their 1974 NBA championship team. He retired after two seasons and is now an associate athletic director at IU. He runs the school's drug and alcohol testing program.

HAVEN'T WE HEARD THIS BEFORE?

Stories suggested Knight had mellowed from his Army days.

"Back then," recalled Tates Lock in an Indianapolis Star story, "he was fiery. Now he's mellowed."

After a 70-69 loss to Ohio State, Knight told the Louisville Times he had toned down his battles with referees.

"When I first started, I had the idea it was a battle each night between myself and the referees. I really think I've gotten away from that. I've found the more officiating you do, the less coaching."

FEISTY AS EVER

Sports Illustrated wrote in a March issue that Knight treated losses to South Carolina and Texas-El Paso "with the grace of a man who has just learned that his bride has been going out with the French Army."

At Texas-El Paso, he got three technical fouls in three

Quinn Buckner was a coach on the floor for Knight.

seconds and was ejected. Stories appeared the next day that Knight had kicked out a window at the Indianapolis airport and that he had thrown a chair into the UTEP crowd. Both were false.

"I guess I came to Indiana without the greatest reputation for sitting quietly," Knight told Sports Illustrated. "I doubt if I'll ever live it down. Whatever I do is magnified. I could become the mildest coach in the world and nobody would believe it. Not even me."

THE 1973-74 SEASON

Future All-Americans Scott May and Kent Benson, plus Bobby Wilkerson, made their debuts, joining Buckner, Green, Laskowski, Tom Abernathy and Crews in a loaded lineup.

May would go on to become the best of the group, although his early catching ability didn't impress Buckner, who called him "stone hands."

MAKING HIS MARK Buckner's 14 assists in a 101-83 victory over Illinois set a Big Ten record.

RUBBER MATCH Indiana rolled to a 12-2 conference mark, tying Michigan for the league championship. That set up a one-game play-off to determine the Big Ten's NCAA participant (conferences could send only one team). The game was played at Champaign, Ill.

The teams had split during the regular season, the Hoosiers losing 73-71 in Ann Arbor and winning 93-81 in Bloomington. This time, the Wolverines won 75-67.

That dropped IU into the Collegiate Commissioners' Association tournament, an event held for major conference runner-ups. The Hoosiers edged Tennessee 73-71 and Toledo 73-72 before meeting Southern California in the finals.

Trailing 28-20 with nine minutes left in the first half, Kent Benson scored seven points in 90 seconds to spur IU to a 40-37 halftime lead. The Hoosiers won 85-60 and finished 23-5, tying the school mark for victories in a season.

Green, who averaged 16.7 points, received his first of two All-American selections. Also averaging in double figures were May (12.5) and Laskowski (12.5). Benson averaged 15.4 points and 11.6 rebounds over his final 10 games. He was named the CCA tourney most valuable player.

NO THANK YOU After the season, a frustrated Knight decided he wasn't getting the job done and offered his resignation. Bill Orwig ignored it.

THE 1974-75 SEASON:

The Hoosiers took the college basketball world by storm. They went 29-0 in the regular season and supplanted UCLA atop the polls. In their regular season finale, an Assembly Hall-record crowd of 17,912 watched the Hoosiers beat Michigan State 94-79.

When asked how to beat the Hoosiers, Ohio State Coach Fred Taylor said you must play Indiana cautiously, "like making love to a porcupine."

Indiana's Scott May. His broken arm in the 1974-75 season may have cost the Hoosiers a national championship.

BAD BREAK Although no one knew it at the time, Indiana's national title hopes ended on Feb. 22, when May broke his left wrist at Purdue. At the time, he was the team's leading scorer with a 19.2 average.

"Toward the end of the half, I don't know ... my hand became numb," May told Inside Indiana. "I don't remember getting hit or twisting it or somebody coming down on me or something.

"I knew at the time something wasn't right. I went to our trainer, Bob Young, and told him I didn't have any feeling in my hand. He sat me down and rotated my wrist ... and I knew that it wasn't good."

STILL FAVORED Even without May, the Big Ten's Most Valuable Player, Indiana was a 9-5 favorite to win NCAA title. UCLA was next at 3-1.

IU opened NCAA Tournament play with victories over Texas-El Paso and Oregon State, extending its victory streak to 34 straight over two seasons. That remains the Big Ten record.

FACING KENTUCKY After missing five straight games, May returned with a brace around his arm. It didn't take long to realize he wasn't ready.

"I played three minutes," said May. "I couldn't do much. I wasn't any help to the team. But if I had been healthy, yeah, it would have made a big difference."

With May during the regular season, IU had beaten the Wildcats 98-74. Without him, despite Benson's 33 points and 23 rebounds, Kentucky won 92-90. The national championship dream was over.

"It still hurts," Steve Green said years later. "You don't forget something like that. Eventually, you get to a level of maturity where it doesn't hurt as much. You accept it because you can't do anything about it. We played as well as we could."

The loss hardened the returning Hoosiers' resolve.

"If you could have been in our locker room afterwards to witness how every player was, that would have been enough for you," said May. "You would have known that we were coming back next year to win it all. ... We didn't want this feeling to ever happen again."

Added Bobby Wilkerson: "We made a commitment that no one was going to beat us next year.

"We would have won it all with May. We probably could have matched back-to-back titles. Looking back at it now, we were that good."

John Laskowski played in the NBA following his career at IU. He now does play-by-play for Indiana games on television.

ON TO THE NBA Green and Laskowski were both drafted. Green was picked in the first round by Chicago in the NBA and Utah in the ABA. Laskowski was Chicago's second-round pick.

Green signed with Utah, a decision that backfired when the team folded two months into the season. Green and teammate Moses Malone were sold to St. Louis of the ABA. There they joined such players as Marvin "Bad News" Barnes, Maurice Lucas, Don Chaney and M.L. Carr. Green later played for the Indiana Pacers before going to dental school. He has his own Indianapolis dental practice.

After playing two years for Chicago, Laskowski entered the real estate business in Indianapolis. He is now the director of marketing and membership for the Indiana Alumni Association and does the play-by-play for IU games on television.

TAKING ON THE MEDIA Knight's first documented media feud started when he tossed a writer from Basketball Weekly out of the locker room following a game.

Then came his battle with Sports Illustrated over a story by writer Curry Kirkpatrick. The story, in Kirkpatrick's trademark smart-aleck style, called Knight a "mellowing maniac" and a "rampaging martinet" and failed to mention any of the Hoosiers' off-court accomplishments. Knight said Kirkpatrick misled him about the story's intent. He threatened to stop talking to the media and cancel his radio and television shows. After calming down, Knight decided not to carry out his threat. However, he did throw Kirkpatrick out of an NCAA Tournament press conference the next time he saw the writer.

THE KENTUCKY INCIDENT Late in IU's 98-74 victory over Kentucky, Knight became incensed over an official's call. While he argued about it, someone on the UK bench – some reports have it as Coach Joe B. Hall, others as a Kentucky assistant coach – shouted "Way to go, Bobby." An angry Knight responded by telling the Wildcats to mind their own business. Hall walked over and told Knight it was just a joke. Both men were smiling. Accepting that, Knight slapped Hall in the back of the head. Knight said later it was a friendly pat. Hall said there was nothing friendly about it and became angry. A Wildcat assistant coach joined the argument before officials broke it up.

"How do I get myself into these things?" Knight later said in Sports Illustrated.

Bob Knight with former Kentucky Coach Joe B. Hall.

THE 1975-76 SEASON

Knight vowed not to dwell on the Kentucky loss.

"What's past is past," he said in a preseason preview. "We can't do anything about last year's team, last year's results or last year's misfortunes. Everyone worked on their games this summer. Buckner (who had given up football the year before) worked harder than he's ever worked before."

THE BIG BANG IU opened by ripping defending national champion

UCLA 84-64 in the Tip-Off Classic in St. Louis. Guard Jim Crews set a school record by recording seven steals.

The record didn't last long. Two months later, May had nine steals in an overtime win over Michigan. He later had a 41-point, 18-rebound performance against Wisconsin.

NICE INCOME An L.A. Times story listed Knight's IU salary at $34,000, which made him one of the nation's highest paid coaches. His outside income generated another $100,000.

THE WISMAN INCIDENT Upset over Jim Wisman's two turnovers against Michigan, Knight grabbed the sophomore by the jersey and jerked him into his seat. Later, Wisman said Knight was right in his actions, but the coach said he was wrong.

Jim Crews helped lead IU to a national championship. He would later become an assistant coach under Knight.

The Indianapolis Star put a photo of Knight grabbing Wisman on its front page. A furious Knight ripped The Star on his TV show. When supportive fans jammed The Stars' telephone switchboard, sports editor Bob Collins printed Knight's unlisted phone number.

"Don't call us," wrote Collins, "call him."

Wisman joked later that Knight "Promised he'd get me a break-away shirt."

OPEN POLICY Despite the media battles, Knight kept his locker room open to the press. That was in contrast to many other Big Ten coaches, including Ohio State's Woody Hayes.

"A reporter has to make a living same as I do," Knight told the Louisville Courier-Journal. "It's part of a player's education to talk to the press."

SUING THE NCAA In December, Knight filed a lawsuit to stop the NCAA from enforcing a new 10- player travel squad rule. Knight said every player should be able to travel. He lost the suit, but the limits were eliminated during the NCAA convention a month later.

PERFECT AGAIN The Hoosiers again went undefeated in the regular season, including a second straight 18-0 mark in the Big Ten. The closest scares were overtime victories against Kentucky (77-68) and Michigan (72-67).

That gave the Hoosiers four straight conference championships and a record 37 consecutive Big Ten victories. The closest any team has come to that mark since is 19.

THE NCAA TOURNAMENT Indiana was healthy and it showed. The Hoosiers beat St. John's 90-70, Alabama 74-69 and Marquette 65-56 to reach the Final Four in Philadelphia. IU won a rematch with UCLA, 65-51, to set up a third meeting with Michigan. The Hoosiers prevailed 86-68 despite an early concussion to Bobby Wilkerson that sent the senior guard to the hospital.

"All I remember is that it happened on a fast break," Wilkerson told Inside Indiana. "I was getting back on defense and there was like a three-on-one break. The guy was going through the air toward the basket. I tried to fake him and move out of the way to deflect the pass.

"As he went up, his elbow went down. He laid the ball on the glass, but his elbow hit me right in the eye. They next thing I remember is waking up in the hospital with my uniform on. A nurse said 'You wouldn't let us take it off.' I remember Coach Knight and John Havlicek coming in the hospital and telling me we had won. I was still halfway out of it.

"I was sad because you work all your college career to win it all and you get to the biggest game of your life and boom – you get hurt. But I felt blessed. It could have been a lot worse. I could have been dead or critically injured."

Bob Wilkerson was a member of IU's 1976 championship team, but he missed most of the title game after suffering a concussion.

SOMETHING SPECIAL "We knew we were a great team," said May. "I'm not sure I thought we were the best team ever, but we were one of the best ever. To go through 32 games and not lose and go through 31 games the year before and not lose …. I knew this was a special group of guys. It was a lot of work and a lot of dedication for not only me, but from everyone else.

"I knew I didn't want to go through what we did in that locker room in 1975. The chemistry was good. Everybody knew their role.

Everybody knew what their job was. There was no bickering and no fighting among ourselves."

As co-captains, May and Buckner saw to that.

"Some guys didn't get a lot of recognition," said May. "But it didn't matter. Buckner was the vocal person on the team. I never said a word, but the guys watched how I practiced and how I played. That was my part. Because every night they saw me playing, they knew what they were going to get.

"We had veteran guys on the bench like Jimmy Crews, who had started on a Final Four team when he was a freshman. The young players could see that here was a guy who started in the Final Four and all of a sudden, he's not playing. But they looked at him. He was involved in the game, he cared about what was happening to his teammates. It was just perfect for what we tried to do."

After the season, May won his second straight Big Ten MVP award and was named the collegiate player of the year. Benson also made All-American and Knight was named national coach of the year.

May averaged 23.5 points. His 752 points was a school single-season record until Calbert Cheaney broke it in 1993 with 785. May's 1,593 points put him second on IU's career list at the time. He is now ninth.

OLYMPIANS That summer, May and Buckner helped the U.S. men's basketball team win the gold medal in Montreal. An injury kept Benson from trying out.

QUITE A DRAFT Four Hoosiers were drafted by NBA teams. May, Buckner and Wilkerson were first-round picks. May, the second overall choice, was taken by the Chicago Bulls. Buckner went to Milwaukee. Wilkerson went to Seattle. It was the first time a college

Scott May (second row, far right) and Quinn Buckner (first row, second from right) were members of the 1976 U.S.A. Olympic Gold Medal team.

team had three No. 1 picks in the same season. Tom Abernathy was a third-round pick of the Los Angeles Lakers.

"You better take one last, long look at this group," Knight told a large IU crowd after the season, "because it's going to be a long time before you see another one that has accomplished what these kids have."

Kent Benson, left, was one of the few bright spots in the 1976-77 season at Indiana. At right Mike Woodson and Coach Bob Knight.

THE 1976-77 SEASON

The Hoosiers returned to earth. Even All-American center Kent Benson and freshman sensation Mike Woodson weren't enough to keep Knight from one of his worst seasons at Indiana. The Hoosiers struggled to a 14-13 record that was later improved to 16-11 when Minnesota forfeited a pair of victories for using an ineligible player.

Benson, who averaged 19.8 points and 10.8 rebounds, became IU's third straight Big Ten MVP. He was the NBA draft's No. 1 pick, going to the Milwaukee Bucks.

Woodson, who had three 30-point games, finished with an 18.5 average.

MOUNTING DEFECTIONS Rich Valavicus and Mike Miday quit the team and publicly criticized Knight.

They were among six defections in the 12 months since IU had won the national championship. The others were Derek Holcomb, Mark Haymore, Bob Bender and Trent Smock.

That didn't hurt recruiting. The incoming freshmen were Indiana Mr. Basketball Ray Tolbert, Steve Risley, Phil Isenbarger and Tommy Baker.

THE 1977-78 SEASON

With Woodson taking charge, Wayne Radford earning All-Big Ten and academic All-American honors, and Tolbert asserting himself, the Hoosiers bounced back for a 21-8 record, 12-6 in the Big Ten. They won 10 of their last 11 regular season games. Only a 1-5 stretch early in the conference season prevented them from winning the championship.

IU received an NCAA bid. The Hoosiers edged Furman 63-62 before losing to Villanova 61-60.

THE BIG BUST While in Alaska for a tournament, Knight heard about a party in which IU players were smoking marijuana. He called each player into his office. In the aftermath, Knight suspended five players – Woodson, Eric Kirchner, Landon Turner, Tolbert and Phil Isenbarger – and kicked Tommy Baker, Jim Roberson and Don Cox off the team.

SILENCE IS GOLDEN Knight boycotted the media. He didn't talk until the NCAA Tournament press conference just before IU's opener against Furman. He said the reason he did speak had nothing to do with NCAA rules, which mandate coaches and designated players from each team address the media.

"I haven't read the NCAA rulebook, so I can't tell you if that's in there or not," Knight said about the NCAA requirement. "But I can tell you if I really didn't want to (talk), I wouldn't be here. I would have to believe that the Bill of Rights supersedes the NCAA rulebook and I think in the Bill of Rights it guarantees the right of free speech. Interpreted broadly, I would think that would include the right to remain silent, if one so chooses."

THE 1978-79 SEASON

Knight added the National Invitation Tournament championship to his resume' when the Hoosiers won the tourney for the first time.

IU struggled during the regular season, finishing 18-12 overall and 10-8 in the Big Ten. But the Hoosiers rebounded in the postseason with victories over Texas Tech (78-59), Alcorn State (73-69) and Ohio State (64-55) to set up a championship meeting with Purdue.

The teams had split during the season, each winning at home. In the title game, Indiana won 53-52 on an 18-foot jumper by Butch Carter in the final seconds.

ANOTHER ALL-AMERICAN Woodson became the Hoosiers' 11th All-American in five seasons. He averaged 21.0 points. That included a 48-point effort against Illinois, the third-highest total in IU history behind Jimmy Rayl's two 56-point games.

"That ranks at the top as one of my career highlights," Woodson told Inside Indiana. "I went into that game really displeased because I hadn't been put on the All-Big Ten first team (by United Press International). I thought I had a good season. After reading that… it wasn't that I planned to go out and score 48 points, but it couldn't

The Hoosiers celebrate winning the 1979 NIT Championship.

have come at a better time."

Added Illinois Coach Lou Henson: "I've never had an opponent score like that against any of my teams. We had our best defensive players on him, and we even gave them help."

The next day, the Associated Press picked Woodson to its all-conference first team.

THE 1979-80 SEASON

With 1,791 points, Woodson entered the season with a shot at breaking Don Schlundt's school career scoring record of 2,192.

But in December, he went down with a herniated back disc. The injury came after a fall during preseason practice. Woodson played six games before leg numbness sent him back to the doctors. His options: don't operate and risk being a cripple; operate and stand a 50-50 chance of never playing again.

Woodson opted for surgery. Amazingly, he was back in eight weeks. He played in the Hoosiers' final eight games as they went 21-8 and won the Big Ten title with a 13-5 mark. They clinched the championship with a 76-73 win over Ohio State in the regular season finale.

"The highlight of my college career was coming back after that surgery," Woodson said. "I was blessed. Dr. Foyer in Indianapolis, who performed the surgery, saved my career. I played my first game in February and never looked back...."

Still, the comeback was hard on him.

"Physically, I just didn't have it when I came back. I was playing on pure guts. I was trying to let people know I could still play."

Despite playing just six Big Ten games, Woodson was named the conference's most valuable player. He finished with 2,061 points, which ranks fourth in school history behind Calbert Cheaney, Steve Alford and Schlundt.

Woodson was a first-round pick of the NBA's New York Knicks. He played 11 pro seasons, averaged 14 points a game and scored more than 10,000 career points.

ANOTHER HONOR Knight was selected as the Big Ten coach of the year, the fourth time in nine years he had received the award.

NCAA TOURNAMENT IU opened with a 68-59 victory over Virginia Tech before losing to Purdue, 76-69. That sent the Boilermakers into the Final Four.

"We beat Purdue in the NIT the year before and they returned the favor the next season," Woodson said. "Not to take anything away from Purdue because they had a good team, but they beat a good team in Indiana."

FIRING AWAY In another controversial incident, Knight playfully fired a blank shot at Louisville Courier-Journal reporter Russ Brown, say-

---

HOT TIMES IN PUERTO RICO

During the 1979 Pan American Games, Knight was charged and later tried and convicted in absentia for hitting a Puerto Rican policeman before a practice session. Knight was sentenced to six months in jail. Not until 1987 did the Puerto Rican government drop efforts to extradite him.

The incident occurred after the Brazilian women's squad arrived in the gym before the U.S. team's practice had ended. Knight's talk with the players was interrupted by noise coming from the women's team. Knight told assistant coach Mike Kryzyewski to ask them to be quiet or leave. Kryzyewski started arguing with a policeman involved with security. Knight got involved and the argument intensified. The policeman poked Knight in the eye. Knight pushed the policeman away, contacting the officer's face with his hand. Knight was then arrested and handcuffed.

Knight described the incident as "a minor argument between two people that should not have gone further." He called the push a "reflex action" after getting hit in the eye. The officer called it "a punch."

The officer's version became less credible when he said Knight called him a "nigger," a term no one believed the coach would use.

However, furious Puerto Rican officials refused to give Knight the benefit of the doubt. Already upset by what he perceived as Knight's earlier insulting actions and comments, Arturo Gallardo, president of the Puerto Rican basketball federation, wrote in a New York Times story that Knight was rude and offensive and that "a different kind of basketball coach" from the "gentlemanly Claire Bee," who had previously coached U.S. teams in Puerto Rico. "What Knight sowed," wrote Gallardo, "the players reaped, and that accounts for the booing of the team."

F. Don Miller of U.S. Olympic Committee executive director said the conviction of Knight was "blaing he did it to keep from going nuts. A week later, Knight and his wife took turns at the microphone and chided the Assembly Hall crowd for not cheering enough during a game against Northwestern.

OLYMPIAN Guard Isiah Thomas, who had just completed his freshman season, was named to the U.S. Olympic team. However, because of the U.S. boycott of the Games, which were held in Moscow, he never got a chance to play.

Isiah Thomas helped lead the Hoosiers to a national championship, then left school two years early to play in the NBA.

tant, outrageous and unwarranted." As the controversy grew, Knight offered to resign as Indiana coach, but school officials refused it.

Criticized for his lack of diplomacy, Knight told the Louisville Courier-Journal that "An international tea is a situation for diplomacy. Basketball is not an international tea. It's competition and we didn't go there to apologize or take any crap off anybody. We went there to beat the (bleep) off nine basketball teams and that's what we did."

Meanwhile, nothing happened to Cuban player Tomas Herrara, who slugged U.S. guard Kyle Macy and broke his jaw in a game.

Woodson led the U.S. in scoring (18.3). Incoming IU freshman Isiah Thomas had 21 points, four assists and five steals in the title victory over Puerto Rico.

The 1979 Pan American Games Gold Medal Team. IU's Mike Woodson (seated, second from left), Ray Tolbert (standing, 4th from left) and incoming freshman Isiah Thomas (seated, center) were among the stars of the team.

THE 1980-81 SEASON

Despite plenty of talent, Indiana struggled early, opening 2-2 and then going 1-2 in Hawaii's Rainbow Classic. Knight was especially frustrated with junior forward Landon Turner, who lacked the concentration and effort the coach demanded. At one point, Knight told Turner to turn pro after the season. After limited action in the next five games, Knight put Turner in against Northwestern, telling him "This is your last chance." Turner responded, making 4-of-5 shots and playing with new-found intensity. That boosted a powerful line-up that already included Isiah Thomas, Ray Tolbert, Randy Wittman, Jim Thomas and Ted Kitchel. Turner went on to reach double figures in nine of his final 11 games.

IU won its last five regular season games to earn its second straight Big Ten crown with a 14-4 mark.

RECORD SHOOTING Kitchel made all 18 of his free throw attempts in a 78-61 victory over Illinois, setting a conference record that still stands.

Ted Kitchel set a Big Ten free throw shooting record while at Indiana which still stands. He now does color commentary for IU games on television.

NCAA TOURNAMENT IU caught fire with routs of Maryland (99-64), Alabama-Birmingham (87-72), St. Joseph's (78-46) and Louisiana State (67-49) to set up a championship matchup with North Carolina.

The Tarheels had beaten the Hoosiers at Chapel Hill during the regular season, 65-56. But an Isiah Thomas-inspired second-half surge lifted Indiana to the national championship.

TRAGEDY STRIKES LANDON TURNER

Knight said Turner was the key in the national championship drive. A rigorous postseason conditioning program had the 6-10, 250-pounder in the best shape of his life as he pre-

Landon Turner

pared for his senior year. He was, Knight believed, poised to become the NBA's No. 1 draft pick the next season.

But it all ended in July of 1981 on a twisting stretch of Ind. 46 near Columbus. On his way to Kings Island in Cincinnati, Turner lost control of his Ford LTD and crashed. Pulled from the bent wreckage, doctors quickly ascertained the bitter truth – Turner had fractured his spine and irreparably damaged his spinal cord. He had become a paraplegic, paralyzed from the chest down.

Knight, who was on a fishing trip in Idaho, rushed back upon hearing the news. A visibly shaken coach told the Courier-Journal shortly after seeing Turner that "Nothing has ever affected me like this. To see that

kid there in that bed.... He was as close to being a totally effective person as he has ever been."

Knight started a fund that eventually raised more than $400,000. He helped motivate Turner to rehabilitate and return to school to get his degree. In a special recognition in the spring of 1982, Turner was voted All-American.

During a tribute to Turner several years later, Knight said he thought Turner would have been the best player in the Big Ten as a senior and perhaps been "as good a player as we would have ever seen at Indiana....

"And yet, I remember how he came back. How he got his degree in 1984 and the things he has done since."

Turner, who once said he would never play wheelchair basketball, eventually did just that. In 1989, the United States Basketball Writers Association voted him its Most Courageous Award.

"The transition wasn't easy," Turner told The Indianapolis Star. "I went through a lot of hard times.... But I didn't want to quit.... Instead of feeling sorry for myself, I can be an inspiration to others."

THE DONKEY SHOW

Knight used his weekly TV program to show highlights of a "sucker punch" incident between Isiah Thomas and Purdue's Roosevelt Barnes, which he said proved Thomas' innocence and showed Barnes provoked the incident.

Critical of the "Purdue mentality" (Purdue officials had reportedly started the Thomas criticism), Knight aggravated Boilermaker fans and officials by bringing a donkey wearing a Purdue cap onto his show. The donkey – Knight said his first name was Jack and "I'll let you figure out his last name" – was a substitute for Purdue Athletic Director George King, who declined to appear on the show. Knight said the donkey "probably would express the same ideas (as King)" and would be "symbolic of Purdue fans."

Upon arriving in Bloomington after winning the national championship, Knight said "We were going to bring Jack back with us, but he was up north (in West Lafayette) visiting his brothers, Half and Wise."

TURNING PRO Thomas, who led Indiana in scoring (16.0) and set a school single-season record for assists (197), gave up his final two years to enter the NBA draft. He was the No. 2 pick overall, going to the Detroit Pistons. He went on to have what will be a Hall of Fame career with two NBA titles. He is in charge of basketball operations for the Toronto Raptors.

Also drafted in the first round was Ray Tolbert, the 18th overall pick by the New Jersey Nets. Tolbert earlier had been named the Big Ten's most valuable player, IU's ninth overall and fifth in seven years.

Knight was once again named the conference's coach of the year.

Bob Knight in 1982.

THE 1981-82 SEASON

Without Thomas and Turner, IU's shot at consecutive national championships disappeared. Indiana endured an early four-game losing streak and was 6-5 at one point. However, with Kitchel earning All-American honors, the Hoosiers rallied to post a 19-10 record and qualified for the NCAA Tournament. Alabama-Birmingham eliminated them in the first round.

THE 1982-83 SEASON

IU went 10-0 in the non-conference for the first time since the 1976 national championship season. After a 70-67 loss at Ohio State, the Hoosiers won five more in a row.

They went on to win the Big Ten title with a 13-5 record, their third crown in four years.

DUKING IT OUT Critical of Big Ten officiating, Knight stood at mid-court cursing at Big Ten Commissioner Wayne Duke, who was sitting in the press box. Two days later, Knight publicly blasted officials for the "worst officiating I have seen in 12 years."

HIGHLIGHTS Randy Wittman, who averaged 18.9 points, was named the conference's most valuable player. He was a first-round pick of the Atlanta Hawks. Also drafted was Jim Thomas, a second-round pick of the Indiana Pacers.... Despite injuries, Ted Kitchel averaged 17.3 points, giving the Hoosiers two of the league's top scorers.... Freshman center Uwe Blab averaged 12.6 points over his last 13 games, and had 12 double-doubles.

Randy Wittman

NCAA TOURNAMENT The Hoosiers opened with a 63-49 victory over Oklahoma at Evansville. Kentucky eliminated them in the next round, 64-59.

THE 1983-84 SEASON

Indiana duplicated its 13-5 Big Ten record of the previous season, but it wasn't enough as Purdue and Illinois shared the conference crown with 15-3 marks. The Hoosiers wound up 22-9.

Dan Dakich gained fame for his defense while at Indiana. He is now an assistant coach for the Hoosiers.

NATIONAL CHAMPION Freshman Steve Alford led the nation in free throw shooting with a 91.3 percentage. He led the Hoosiers with a 15.5 scoring average.

NCAA TOURNAMENT A 75-67 victory over Richmond set up an encounter with Michael Jordan-led North Carolina. With Dan Dakich gaining lasting fame for his defensive performance against Jordan, IU upset the top-ranked Tar Heels, 72-68. Jordan, the college player of the year, finished 6-for-14 from the field for 13 points.

"All I told Dakich," Knight said after the game, "was 'Just don't let him dunk on you. That'll embarrass you and me.'"

The Hoosiers ran out of steam two days later against Virginia, losing 50-48 and missing a spot in the Final Four.

OLYMPIANS Knight and Alford helped the U.S. win the Olympic gold medal in Los Angeles. The team, led by Michael Jordan (Knight called him "the best that will ever play the game.") and Patrick Ewing, routed the field. Hoosier center Uwe Blab played for the West German squad.

Knight had prepared for the Olympics for two years, saying the opportunity was one of the highmarks of his career. "The prospect of coaching the Olympic team excites me about as much as anything I've ever done," he told the Indianapolis Star a month before the Games started. He also denied preparations were affecting his IU performance. "I really don't think there has been a drain on me because of that."

In July, a few weeks before the Olympics started, a Hoosier Dome

Steve Alford playing for the U.S.A. Olympic team before a crowd of nearly 70,000 in the Hoosier Dome.

crowd of 67,596 watched an exhibition between the U.S. team and a group of NBA all-stars. It was the largest crowd ever to see a game in the United States.

THE 1984-85 SEASON

Not even a second-place finish in the NIT could wipe out the bad taste of a 19-14 season. It remains the most losses of Knight's career. The 7-11 conference mark was his first losing Big Ten season.

"We were ranked No. 5 in the nation when the season started, and by the end, we were probably rated No. 200," former player Steve Eyl told Inside Indiana.

Knight denied the poor showing was the result of exhaustion from the Olympic effort. However, he responded by renewing his recruiting emphasis.

THE CHAIR Knight gained lasting infamy by tossing a chair early in a game against Purdue at Assembly Hall. Knight's toss came just as Purdue guard Steve Reid was set to shoot a pair of free throws following a technical. Officials immediately ejected Knight. Big Ten Commissioner Wayne Duke suspended Knight, who responded with the following statement:

"Over the years, I've had to make a lot of decisions, as has anyone who is the head of an organization. Just as I believe it is my right and obligation to make decisions that affect my basketball team, so is it Wayne Duke's right and obligation to make decisions he feels affect the Big Ten. I'm glad to see him make a decision....

"When a decision such as this is made, the issue is not whether I agree or disagree, but which of two alternatives do I choose to take: either I accept the decision or I stop coaching at Indiana, and I certainly plan to be coaching here for a long time."

Later, Knight would joke about the incident. To one audience, he said "Most of you do not have a place in history, but I do. I've earned my niche by doing more for the chair than anyone in history." He also said he threw the chair when he heard a grandmotherly woman on the other side of the court, seeing him standing up, shout that if he wasn't going to use the chair, could he give it to her. He obliged.

ANOTHER ALFORD MARK The sophomore guard made 93.5 percent (58-of-62) of his free throws to set a conference record that still stands. He averaged a team-high 18.1 points.

KNIGHT TALES

Over the years, Knight-inspired stories have acquired legend status. Some are true. Some are embellished. Here are a few of the best:

■ Michigan State coach Jud Heathcote remembered once getting a phone call from Knight.

"Bob said, 'Jud, I have to talk to you. You're the only coaching friend I have in the conference.' I said, 'Hey Bob, don't jump to any conclusions.' "

■ Former player John Laskowski told Indianapolis Monthly about a practice from the mid-1970s. The Hoosiers were running wind sprints and Knight, then in his early 30s, wasn't impressed with the effort. He told the players "I can beat some of you guys."

"So he gets on the line and we take off," Laskowski said. "Coach is running as fast as he can, but he gets to the 10-second line and pulls a hamstring. Everybody was able to beat him and he limped across the line. He never did run any more wind sprints with us."

■ During his playing days, Steve Alford had a love-hate relationship with Knight. Alford was famous for glaring at Knight when the coach chewed him out, a silent form of protest that often further angered Knight.

Still, Knight's intimidating manner took its toll. Alford later recalled one incident when he was in his car in Bloomington and saw Knight stopped at a stoplight. Rather than pull up beside him, Alford turned onto a side street.

"It's hard to explain unless you experience it, but some days you just didn't have the energy to face him," he said.

■ Tom Abernathy, who played on the 1976 national championship team, told Indianapolis Monthly about a practice when an irate Knight kicked a ball toward the Assembly Hall ceiling.

"It sailed way up in the air – (Indianapolis Colts punter) Rohn Stark would have been proud of it – and it landed right in a trash basket," Abernathy said of the million-to-one shot. "All of us sort of glanced at the ball and most saw it go in. We started to chuckle and Coach even had a little laugh about it. It saved a pretty tense moment."

■ Ted Kitchel, another former

AROUND-THE-WORLD TOUR Over the summer, Knight took his team on a tour that included stops in Canada, China, Japan, Yugoslavia and Finland against various international teams, including the Soviet Union and the Netherlands. IU finished 12-6 and won its final 10 games.

The Hoosiers lost twice to the Russians, who had boycotted the '84 Olympics. Before the first game, during a gift exchange, Knight gave the Soviet coach a pair of Nike "Air Jordan" shoes with a note that said "Compliments of Bob Knight and the Indiana University basketball team on behalf of the 1984 U.S. Olympic team."

player, once couldn't play or practice because of a deep thigh bruise. He was in the stands watching practice when Knight came by, got in his face and said that John Havlicek played with two thigh bruises. After Knight left, Kitchel began to laugh. What, teammate Phil Isenbarger wanted to know, was Kitchel laughing at?

"If you were Fred Taylor, who would you want to start, an injured John Havlicek or Bob Knight?"

■ Then there was the time Knight asked Uwe Blab to teach him some German swear words. Blab declined, saying "Then you'd know what I'm calling you in practice."

■ During a fundraiser in the late 1980s, Knight talked about helping young children and asked, "Did you ever see a bad 4-year-old kid?"

"Your mother did," quipped former Indianapolis Star sports editor Bob Collins to bring down the house.

■ In a Washington Post story, an unnamed friend joked that Knight is "The meanest sumbitch on two wheels." Later, another unnamed friend said, "Remember, under that surface veneer of

meanness lies a really thick layer of more meanness."

■ Knight addressed his own popularity and image in Esquire. Knight said "I guess maybe people are attracted... to a no-bullshit guy who tells people to shove it up their ass when he thinks it's appropriate."

■ Former referee Charlie Fouty remembered, in a Bloomington Herald-Times story, his first encounter with Knight when the coach was at Army. During a game against Florida State, he called Knight's center for a 3-second violation. Knight responded with a few choice words. When Knight wouldn't stop, Fouty said "All right young man, I'll tell you what I'll do. You tell your center he can sit in that lane all night. We won't be calling 3-second violations. Now I'll go down there and tell that red-headed kid the same thing."

The red-head was center Dave Cowens, a future Hall of Famer. Knight paused, grinned and said, "Aw hell, let's just play the game."

Bob Knight with author John Feinstein during a practice in January of 1986.

THE 1985-86 SEASON

Sports writer John Feinstein joined the Hoosiers for a book project. Knight gave him unlimited access and Feinstein took full advantage. The next year, his "A Season On The Brink" became a national best seller. It remains the best-selling sports book of all time.

Indiana, meanwhile, bounced back with a 21-8 record, 13-5 in the Big Ten. The Hoosiers were second in the Big Ten, one game behind Michigan. They lost the title in the last game when the Wolverines beat them 83-52.

MORE FIREWORKS Knight received a technical foul for shouting at the officials during a game against Illinois, then kicked a megaphone and chewed out the Indiana cheerleaders for disrupting an Alford free throw attempt.

NCAA TOURNAMENT A good season ended on a disappointing note with a stunning 83-79 loss to Cleveland State in the first round. The Hoosiers never adjusted to Cleveland State's pressing, intense, go-for-broke style.

Alford, who averaged 22.5 points and shot 55.6 percent from the field, made All-American. Rick Calloway earned Big Ten and national freshman of the year honors. Undersized center Daryl Thomas averaged 14.6 points and 4.8 rebounds.

THE 1986-87 SEASON

"A Season On the Brink" came out and Knight was not happy. The book included raw language – opening with a vulgar, merciless tirade at Daryl Thomas – Knight believed would never appear in print. Other revelations included Knight's supposed negative comments about Notre Dame Coach Digger Phelps and others. Knight spent much of the season explaining himself and admitted to his players he had made their job more difficult.

Although there was no signed contract, Knight indicated he gave three conditions for allowing Feinstein to do the book: the F-word was not to be used, the book was supposed to focus on the players and the program and not on him, and there was to be no mention of his personal life. Only the last condition was followed.

BIG TEN NO-SHOW In the fall, Knight failed to attend the Big Ten's annual preseason basketball press conference in Chicago, the fourth time in five years he hadn't shown up. When conference officials asked for an explanation, Knight responded with a letter that indicated copies had been sent to Mickey Mouse, Bugs Bunny, Garfield, Pogo, Supreme Court Chief Justice William Rehnquist, former FBI Director William Webster, the National Security Council, Philippines President Corazon Aquino and Illinois Athletic Director Neale Stoner.

In the letter, Knight said he had two questions; "1) If a person would be sick and unable to attend the press conference, how much prior notice does he have to give to your office indicating that he knows he is going to be sick? 2) If a person becomes sick without being able to give sufficient prior notice, would a letter from his mother be satisfactory for his absence.... P.S. Would you send me a list of the meetings that faculty representatives and athletic directors are required to attend. Also, please send me a list of those in each group who have been reprimanded for not attending those meetings."

Knight later refused to participate in the Big Ten's weekly teleconference.

Also, Knight was the only conference coach to vote against a postseason league tourney. The measure was later rejected by faculty representatives.

A JUCO APPROACH For the first time, Knight dipped into the junior college ranks for center Dean Garrett and guard Keith Smart. The 6-10 Garrett was the California junior college player of the year after averaging 19.9 points, nine rebounds and 5.5 blocks for San Francisco Junior College. Smart, with a 40-inch vertical jump, averaged 21.9 points, 8.1 rebounds and 4.4 assists for Garden City Junior College in Kansas. The move paid instant dividends.

In the season opener, Garrett set a school record by blocking eight shots in a 90-55 win over Montana State. He would also block eight shots against Iowa the next season and set school records for blocks with 93 in 1987 and 99 in '88.

Junior college transfer Dean Garrett set a school record for blocked shots while at Indiana.

Smart, of course, would go on to hit one of the biggest shots in NCAA Tournament history.

HIGHLIGHTS Alford made seven 3-pointers in a 103-65 victory over Wisconsin.... Smart set a school record with 15 assists in a 107-90 NCAA Tournament victory over Auburn.... IU beat Ohio State 90-81 in the season finale to clinch a share of the Big Ten title with Purdue. Both had 15-3 league records.

NO MORE LATE STARTS The Big Ten's TV contract with ESPN included 9:30 p.m. starts. After the Hoosiers didn't return home until 3 the next morning following one such game at Wisconsin, an 86-85 triple-overtime victory for the Hoosiers, Knight had enough.

"This Monday night television is just absolute bullshit," he said after the game. "...If the people in the conference can't think enough of the kids to get them in a situation to miss as little class as possible ... It's time the university presidents or somebody stepped in and laid down some rules on when teams can play and when they can't and how much class they're allowed to miss. To hell with ESPN or whatever it is and getting on television. This is absolutely ridiculous to put a college student through."

Knight's comments had their effect. The Big Ten later reworked the contract to avoid late starts.

Daryl Thomas made the pass that led to Keith Smart's winning shot in the NCAA Championship game.

NCAA TOURNAMENT The Hoosiers opened with impressive wins over Fairfield (92-58), Auburn (107-90) and Duke (88-82).

In the regional final against LSU, Indiana rallied from nine points down in the closing minutes for a 77-76 victory. During the game, after getting a technical foul, Knight banged his fist on the scorer's table. The university was fined $10,000 and Knight received a reprimand. It would not be his last.

Knight and LSU Coach Dale Brown got into a war of words. Brown called Knight "A despicable human being" and added, in a bizarre statement, "I'd love to wrestle him naked in a room and see who comes out."

When asked to comment on that, Knight replied, "When you ask questions about him, you should direct them to a psychiatrist, not me." Later, Knight added, "As long as the Dale

Steve Alford was an All-American and Big Ten MVP in the 1987 season.

Browns of the world are in disagreement with me, then I think I'm in pretty good shape." Finally, after beating LSU, Knight said he thought the Hoosiers were in danger of losing "Until I looked at the other bench and saw Dale Brown."

In the Final Four, the Hoosiers faced favored Nevada-Las Vegas. Deciding a deliberate pace wouldn't work against the Rebels' fierce full-court pressure, Knight had IU run at every opportunity. With Alford scoring 33 points, IU won 97-93.

In the championship game against Syracuse, Alford set an NCAA record by making seven 3-point baskets. However, it took Smart's dramatic jumper in the final seconds for the Hoosiers (30-4) to survive, 74-73. It was their fifth national title and third under Knight.

HONORS Alford was named the Big Ten's MVP and made All-American. He broke Don Schlundt's career scoring record, finishing with a then-school record 2,438 points.

"I'll tell you a remarkable thing about Alford and I think the most remarkable thing," Knight said in the IU media guide. "He's not big;

he's not strong; and he's not quick; and he has just scored a ton of points. It's hard for me to imagine how a kid like that can score as many points as he does. He doesn't post up; he doesn't get rebound baskets; and he really doesn't take the ball to the basket to score. He's just got to work like hell to get the jump shot. He's about as good a scorer for being strictly a jump shooter as anybody I've ever seen."

Knight was named the Naismith Coach of the Year. IU led the nation in 3-point percentage, shooting .508. It is a record that still stands.

MOVING ON Alford was a second-round pick by the NBA's Dallas Mavericks. After four years as a reserve, Alford became the head coach at tiny Manchester College in Indiana. In 1995, after leading Manchester to a runner-up finish in the NCAA Division III tournament, Alford became the head coach at Southwest Missouri State, a member of the Missouri Valley Conference.

THE 1987-88 SEASON

Controversy erupted during an exhibition game at Assembly Hall against the Soviet Union. Referees ignored a series of rules violations by the Russians. When Knight protested a call against the Hoosiers,

CONNIE CHUNG AND NEW MEXICO

In an April TV interview with NBC's Connie Chung, when asked how he handled stress, Knight replied "I think that if rape is inevitable, relax and enjoy it." Knight explained he was using a metaphor about a coach's helplessness in dealing with poor officiating, and not the act of rape. He asked NBC not to use the rape remark. The network did use it, and the comment triggered anti-Knight demonstrations and a march of about 300 people on the IU campus. Critical stories appeared in publications and TV commentaries across the country. All that led to:

THE NEW MEXICO SCARE It started in May. New Mexico officials, looking for a new coach and having just been turned down by Purdue's Gene Keady, contacted Knight for recommendations.

They asked Knight if he was interested. He said he was. An avid hunter and fisherman, New Mexico's outdoor opportunities appealed to him.

It wasn't the first opportunity for Knight. In the early 1980s, he was offered jobs with the Arizona Wildcats and the Boston Celtics (Red Auerbach remains a good friend). Before that he considered an offer to do color commentary for CBS.

Word leaked out when Knight visited the New Mexico campus. More than 2,500 people gathered near Assembly Hall to show their support and ask him to stay. A full-page ad appeared in the Bloomington Herald-Times supporting him. Gov. Robert Orr said he hoped Knight would stay.

Knight said financial terms would not affect his decision. "It's a personal decision. I'll have to he wound up with three technical fouls and was ejected. When he refused to leave, officials called the game. With nobody around to explain what had happened, it appeared Knight had pulled his team off the floor. He was reprimanded by the university, which released a statement saying Knight "Had made a serious mistake of judgment" and his actions caused "great embarrassment not only to himself and the basketball program, but also and most importantly, to the entire university and its supporters."

HIGHLIGHTS Led by Smart, Dean Garrett and freshman Jay Edwards, Indiana finished 19-10 overall and 11-7 in the Big Ten.... In a 91-85 victory over Minnesota, Smart made 12-of-14 free throws and extended his consecutive free throw streak to a conference-record 37. Also, Jay Edwards made eight 3-point baskets to break Alford's conference mark of seven.... Edwards was named Big Ten Freshman of the Year. His 3-point percentage of .536 was a freshman NCAA record.

NCAA TOURNAMENT Richmond came out strong and never backed down in a 72-69 upset victory. Smart missed a jumper with 20 seconds left that would have given IU the lead, and possibly the victory.

leave it at that. I'm not going to get into the whys or wherefores." An earlier Knight comment about "changes here that affect things and affect thinking" led many to believe there was friction between he and IU President Thomas Ehrlich.

At the time, Knight reportedly earned $95,400 a year at IU, far more in endorsements, speaking engagements, TV and radio shows, and his basketball camp. New Mexico reportedly offered a five-year deal worth $350,000 annually, plus a $150,000 house. Lobos officials said they would match anything IU offered.

Knight insisted the perceived lack of support from Ehrlich (who had called Knight's rape comments "coarse" and in "poor taste," and disassociated the university from it) had nothing to do with the situation. Ehrlich said he wanted Knight to stay.

Concern arose that Knight's possible departure would affect incoming recruits. Chesteron (Ind.) High School senior Matt Nover said in wire service reports that, "I'd hate to think of him not being there. That would be terrible. It would definitely change my thinking (about coming to IU)." Another recruit, Eric Anderson, said he'd come to IU regardless.

After two weeks, Knight decided to stay and New Mexico picked former IU assistant Dave Bliss. In explaining his decision, Knight said he didn't want to expend the energy necessary to get the program to a nationally competitive level.

Ehrlich expressed his happiness with Knight's decision. He said Knight had not been treated fairly by NBC and that he would not have criticized Knight if he had known all the facts.

"This is where we believe Bob Knight belongs," said Ehrlich. "This is his home."

THE 1988-89 SEASON

Indiana was rocked early. During the Big Apple NIT, Syracuse and North Carolina torched the IU defense for more than 100 points in consecutive games, the first time that had ever happened. A week later, Louisville also broke the 100-point barrier. That dropped the Hoosiers' record to 3-4.

Indiana responded with a 13-game winning streak and victories in 21 of its next 22 games. Jay Edwards was a miracle man, hitting last-second shots to beat Purdue (74-73) and Michigan (76-75). He nearly did the same thing against Illinois until Nick Anderson buried an almost half-court 3-pointer at the buzzer for an Illini victory.

The Hoosiers went on to win the Big Ten championship with a 15-3 record.

SECOND TO NONE Knight became the Big Ten's winningest coach, topping the 213 victories by Purdue's Ward "Piggy" Lambert. Knight passed him with a 74-73 win at Purdue.

NCAA TOURNAMENT IU opened with victories over George Mason (99-85) and Texas-El Paso (92-69) before losing to eventual national runner-up Seton Hall, 78-65.

HONORS Edwards, who averaged 20 points and shot 44.8 percent from 3-point range, was named All-American. He gave up his final two years of eligibility to enter the NBA draft. He was a second-round choice of the Los Angeles Clippers.... Knight was selected as national coach of the year.... The Hoosiers led the nation in 3-point shooting, at 47.3 percent.

THE 1989-90 SEASON

Freshmen Calbert Cheaney, Greg Graham, Indiana Mr. Basketball Pat Graham, Chris Reynolds, Lawrence Funderburke, Chris Lawson and Todd Leary arrived, giving Knight one of his all-time best recruiting classes. With eight of the top nine scorers freshmen or sophomores, it was Knight's youngest-ever team.

The freshmen led IU to a 10-0 start before running into Big Ten reality. The Hoosiers' 8-10 league mark was just the second time a Knight team finished below .500. Indiana ended its season with a 65-63 loss to California in an NCAA Tournament opener.

MISSING IN ACTION Just before the Dec. 16 game at Texas-El Paso, Funderburke disappeared. He had been thrown out of practice and never returned. A few days later, he was seen watching a high school game in Henderson, Ky. He eventually tried to return to the team. Knight refused to let him, saying he "wasn't a social worker." Funderburke ended up at Ohio State.

HIGHLIGHTS Cheaney led the team in scoring with a 17.1 average.... Sophomore Eric Anderson averaged 16.3 points and a team-high 7.0 rebounds.... Pat Graham averaged 12.8 points in his final 12 games and made his last 28 free throws.

The 1989-90 Indiana squad featured one of the top recruiting classes in school history.

As a Freshman, Calbert Cheaney led the Hoosiers in scoring. He would eventually become the Big Ten's all-time leading scorer.

THE 1990-91 SEASON

The Hoosiers went 29-5 and shared the Big Ten title with Ohio State. Both had 15-3 records.

Cheaney improved on his strong freshman numbers by averaging 21.6 points and shooting a school-record 59.6 percent from the field.

DAMON'S DEBUT After a sensational prep career, Damon Bailey arrived on campus. He had a solid year – 11.4 scoring average, 50.6 field goal shooting – as a support player to Cheaney.

FREE THROW RECORD Pat Graham made all four free throw attempts against Notre Dame. That gave him a school record 38 in a row.

HIGHLIGHTS IU finished second in the season-opening Maui Classic, losing to Syracuse 77-74 in the finals ... It won 10 straight to open the Big Ten season at 12-1 ... Despite Bailey's 32 points, Ohio State beat the Hoosiers 97-95 in double overtime in

Damon Bailey came to Indiana after being named USA Today's high school player of the decade.

Columbus ... Eric Anderson joined Cheaney on the All-Big Ten team after averaging 13.7 points and 7.1 rebounds.

TAKING ON LOU After a victory at Illinois, Knight and Illini Coach Lou Henson had a heated exchange during which Henson called him a "classic bully" and Knight made a variety of sarcastic comments

Bob Knight with fellow Hall of Fame inductees Harry Gallatin (left), Dave Cowens, and Nate "Tiny" Archibald.

about Henson and the Illinois program. The Big Ten reprimanded both coaches, who later reconciled.

A HALL OF FAMER Knight was inducted into the Basketball Hall of Fame. After failing to receive enough votes in his first year of eligibility, Knight said he didn't want to be considered anymore. The selection committee did anyway.

NCAA TOURNAMENT The Hoosiers got some much needed 3-point shooting from Pat Graham to beat Coastal Carolina in the opener, then took out a strong Florida State team, 82-60. That set up a showdown with Kansas. The Jayhawks jumped to an early 19-point lead and the Hoosiers never recovered, losing 83-65.

THE 1991-92 SEASON

In the season-opening Tip-Off Classic, UCLA routed the Hoosiers 87-72 as Cheaney was held to eight points on 2-of-9 shooting. That typified an inconsistent season for the junior forward, who found himself on the bench, the recipient of one of Knight's favorite motivational tools.

Still, IU won. A 13-game winning streak boosted the Hoosiers toward the top of the polls. They twice beat Ohio State, their biggest challenger for the conference crown. They entered the season finale at Purdue tied with the Buckeyes for the Big Ten lead. A victory would give them at least a share of the league crown and the No. 1 seed in the Midwest Regional in Cincinnati.

Knight made news conferences interesting during the 1992 NCAA Tournament, at one point turning the tables and asking reporters questions.

MORE CONTROVERSY Indiana blew it all with a 61-59 loss to Purdue, losing a 10-point lead in the final minutes. The loss made IU an NCAA Tournament second seed and sent the Hoosiers to Boise, Idaho, and the West Regional.

The next day, Knight created an uproar by canceling the annual team banquet. He said the timing was coincidence, that it had nothing to do with the loss. Few believed him. Knight didn't help matters when, while defending the decision, he indicated it was a banquet the players didn't want to attend, anyway.

A week later, while practicing in Albuquerque for a West Regional semifinal game against Florida State, Knight found himself in more hot water after playfully giving a mock whipping to Cheaney, a black player. It was meant as a joke over his reputation as a taskmaster. Local and national black leaders didn't see the humor and demanded an apology. Knight denied any racial connotations. Cheaney said it was blown out of proportion. Most members of the media defended Knight against charges of racism.

Meanwhile, Knight reacted to the controversies by filibustering through NCAA press conferences with talk of cerebral reversal, Chinese water torture and team campouts. He talked about making players sleep in the parking lot, turning fire hoses on them every couple of hours. He said he stuck their feet in buckets of ice water, chained them, starved them, whipped them. At one point, he brought a whip his son Patrick had given him, dipping its tip in water as he spoke because, he said, that improved its effectiveness.

In one hilarious session, Knight graded reporters' questions, saying he was writing a story for the New Yorker. One reporter started his question by saying he was going to take up fishing, one of Knight's favorite activities.

"You've got an A-plus right there," said Knight. "Do you want to stay there or do you want to go for more? Remember, more is usually less."

It was less. The reporter asked what he could do to improve his jump shot.

"It looks like you're down to a D with that one," Knight said.

NCAA TOURNAMENT After the Purdue loss, Knight stripped Eric Anderson and Jamal Meeks of their co-captainship and gave it to Cheaney. He also started Matt

Todd Leary's 3-point barrage in the final minute nearly helped IU defeat Duke in the NCAA Tournament semi-finals.

Nover and Chris Reynolds in place of Anderson and Meeks. The Hoosiers responded with victories over Eastern Illinois, Louisiana State (besting center Shaquille O'Neal in his final college game) and Florida State to set up a rematch with UCLA.

The Hoosiers routed the Bruins 106-79 victory to advance to their seventh Final Four. It was UCLA's worst NCAA Tournament loss ever. Cheaney led all scorers with 23 points.

IU then faced defending national champion Duke and its coach, former Knight player Mike Kryzewski. The Hoosiers opened an early 12-point lead, then fell victim to foul trouble and Bobby Hurley's 3-point shooting. Still, Indiana nearly pulled it out when Todd Leary came off the bench (by then Cheaney, Alan Henderson, Greg Graham and Damon Bailey had fouled out) to hit three 3-point baskets in the final minute. Duke prevailed 81-78 when Jamal Meeks' 3-point attempt bounced off the rim.

WRAPPING IT UP The Hoosiers' 27-7 record was the fifth-highest victory total in school history. IU outscored opponents by 17.6 points to lead the nation.

THE 1992-93 SEASON

Ranked No. 1 for most of the season, the Hoosiers' national title hopes took a huge hit in February when Alan Henderson tore a ligament in his knee. He missed the final six games of the regular season and saw limited action in the NCAA Tournament. IU also played much of the way without Pat Graham, who rebroke the same bone in his right foot that had sidelined him the previous year.

However, with Cheaney on a college player-of-the-year pace, Indiana rolled to the Big Ten title with a 17-1 record. The only loss came 81-77 in overtime at Ohio State.

HIGHLIGHTS Cheaney scored 36 points to lead IU over Seton Hall 78-74 in the Pre-Season NIT championship game at New York's Madison Square Garden ... Greg Graham made 26 of 28 free throws against Purdue at Assembly Hall to set conference records for most free throws made and attempted in a game. He finished with 32 points ... Greg Graham's 32 points led the Hoosiers to a 99-68 win over Michigan State to clinch Indiana's 19th Big Ten title and 11th under Knight. Cheaney passed Jay Edwards for the school record by getting his 141st career 3-point basket. He finished with 148.... Cheaney was the consensus Big Ten MVP and college player of the year.

ESPN's Dick Vitale talks with Calbert Cheaney following the Pre-Season NIT championship game.

NCAA TOURNAMENT As the top seed in the Midwest, the Hoosiers opened with a

CHEANEY SETS SCORING RECORD

On March 4 against Northwestern, in front of a sell-out Assembly Hall crowd, Cheaney became the Big Ten's all-time leading scorer.

He entered the game with 2,433 points, five behind Steve Alford, six behind Michigan's Mike McGee and nine behind Michigan's Glenn Rice.

Cheaney wasted no time passing Alford and McGee, needing just 68 seconds to score IU's first seven points.

"I was so nervous," he said. "I hit those first three shots and I was shaking."

Cheaney passed Rice with a 3-point basket with 6:09 left in the first half.

"It's been a great privilege to play with Calbert," said teammate and roommate Chris Reynolds. "We take Calbert for granted sometimes because we see him every day, but he's the best player in the Big Ten. I've never seen a better scorer."

Cheaney scored 35 points in the game. He finished his career with 2,613 points.

"This is a great honor for a great kid," said Knight. "I don't think there's ever been a more deserving kid.

"He's able to score in every way possible. Probably nobody we've had has been as versatile a scorer as Calbert.

"He can do a little bit of everything. He can shoot; he's quick enough to get past you; and he can play in the post. He does everything better than everybody else.

"The next honor for him should be Player of the Year in the Big Ten, and it should be unanimous. Then, he should get Player of the Year nationally."

Cheaney fires the shot that puts him in the record book at the Big Ten's all-time leading scorer.

97-54 rout of Wright State. Xavier gave them all they wanted before falling 73-70. Against Louisville, Cheaney's 32 points paced Indiana to an 82-69 victory. That setup a rematch with Kansas.

The Jayhawks had beaten Indiana earlier in the season, 74-69, at the Hoosier Dome. Without a healthy Henderson, the Hoosiers couldn't handle Kansas' inside power. The Jayhawks won 83-77 to advance to the Final Four. IU finished 31-4.

ON TO THE NBA Cheaney was the sixth overall pick in the draft by the Washington Bullets. He signed a six-year, $18 million contract. Greg Graham was the 17th pick by the Charlotte Hornets, although he was soon traded to the Philadelphia 76ers.

THE 1993-94 SEASON

BAD BEGINNING Butler stunned the seventh-ranked Hoosiers 75-71 at Hinkle Fieldhouse. Bulldogs guard Travis Trice, a former Purdue reserve, killed IU with seven 3-point baskets. That led to one of the most intense weeks of practice ever under Knight.

BOUNCING BACK Indiana responded with a thrilling 96-84 victory over No. 1 Kentucky before 38,197 at the Hoosier Dome. The Hoosiers were led by Damon Bailey's 29 points that included six crucial free throws down the stretch. The performance put him on the cover of Sports Illustrated.

Damon Bailey had an outstanding game in the Hoosiers upset of top-ranked Kentucky. The effort landed him on the cover of Sports Illustrated.

"This is the best I've ever seen Bailey play," said Knight. "This is how I think he has to play; this is how I think he's capable of playing.

"There was something about Bailey today that said, 'We're going to play.' I'm not sure, except in spurts, that I've ever seen that before. Whether he's able to sustain it, that's the next question."

HIGHLIGHTS IU opened 3-0 in the Big Ten following an 82-72 victory over Michigan. Alan Henderson (19 points, 16 rebounds), Brian Evans (14 and 15) and Todd Leary (career-high 16 points) led the way ... Evans played most of the season with a dislocated shoulder. It required postseason surgery ... Leary made his first five free throws against Minnesota to give him a record 46 in a row in Big Ten action over four years ... Bailey scored a career-high 33 points in a 93-91 win over Iowa ... Henderson scored a career-high 41 points in a 94-78 loss at Michigan State.

THE KICKING INCIDENT Late in a 19-point victory over Notre Dame at Assembly Hall, just days after the Kentucky game solidified his genius reputation, Knight returned to the dark side of the force. Furious with son Patrick over an errant pass, the elder Knight called a timeout, flung a warmup into the air, shoved his son into a chair and, during a tongue-lashing, appeared to kick Patrick in the leg. Amazingly, fans sitting above and behind the bench booed and shouted. Bob Knight responded by cursing at the crowd, telling them, in so many words, to get out. School officials suspended him for the next game and publications across the country demanded he be fired.

Knight issued a statement after the suspension was announced: "If my reaction to the jeering from the stands on Tuesday night offended any true Hoosier fans, I am deeply sorry and wish to apologize.

"I realize that you have not always agreed with what I have done or said. Given the opportunity to observe each of you, I probably wouldn't agree with all that any of you said or did, either.

"I also realize I have made mistakes over the years in a variety of ways, which once again doesn't make me any different from most of you."

Knight later indicated to a reporter he was suspended for cursing at the crowd, and not the kick. He denied kicking his son.

"How many times have you seen me yell at a player?" he said in the Indianapolis Star. "God can't count that many times. Now, how many times have you ever seen me yell at people in the stands? Never. So that's a different thing....What I haven't seen is a coach yell at the crowd, which I admittedly did, and I think that separates the issue from anything else."

Later, Knight and guard Sherron Wilkerson banged heads during a game at Michigan State. That generated more criticism. Knight insisted it was an accident caused by his injured back. Wilkerson later supported Knight, saying "The thing was totally blown out of proportion.... I'm telling you this, if Coach Knight were to leave, I would leave right behind him."

Knight got in the last word after the regular season finale with a

Coach Knight on the bench with his son Pat, an alleged kicking victim.

vulgar verse directed at his critics, saying that he wanted to be buried
upside down so critics could kiss his posterior end.

THE MINNESOTA DEBACLE The injury riddled Hoosiers were no match
for Minnesota at Williams Hall. Trailing by 22 points at halftime,
Knight elected to not to play Bailey, Evans and Henderson in the
final 20 minutes. The result was a 106-56 loss, the worst ever under
Knight. Upset fans couldn't understand Knight's tactics (he wanted
to rest the players, specifically Bailey, for the upcoming grueling
stretch of games) given that Kentucky, just a week earlier, had rallied
from a bigger deficit against Louisiana State.

ANOTHER SWEET 16 Indiana won its first two NCAA Tournament
games, including a 67-58 upset over favored Temple, to make the
Sweet 16 for the fourth straight season. The Temple win was costly
when Wilkerson broke his leg in the second half. Boston College
ended the Hoosiers' season the next game with a 77-68 victory.

GOODBYE DAMON Bailey ended his career as the fifth-best scorer in IU
history with 1,741 points (Alan Henderson passed him in 1995).
Bailey was picked in the second round by the Indiana Pacers. Surgery
to both knees forced him to miss all of the 1994-95 NBA season.

THE 1994-95 SEASON

IU opened 2-4, the worst start ever under Knight. However, the Hoosiers rebounded to finish 19-12, 11-7 in the Big Ten, and qualified for the NCAA Tournament for the 10th straight season. They set a school record by extending their homecourt winning streak to 50 games before Michigan ended it in late January. The streak started in February of 1991.

Turnovers hurt Indiana all season. A big reason was the loss of Sherron Wilkerson, who never recovered from surgery to repair his broken leg. That gave the Hoosiers little experience at guard, a weakness opponents exploited.

STRONG FRESHMEN Andrae Patterson, Neil Reed, Michael Hermon, Charlie Miller and Rob Hodgson were highly touted. The 6-9 Patterson was considered one of the nation's top prep players as a senior, while the 6-3 Reed was also a McDonald's All-American.

Patterson and Reed had their moments, although both suffered injuries. Reed was hindered by a dislocated shoulder that required off-season surgery. Patterson missed three games with a knee injury.

Hermon, one of the biggest freshman contributors, caused a stir by leaving the team in early December. Knight gave him a second chance and Hermon responded with some solid performances. However, he began missing classes and postseason conditioning sessions. He was voted off the team and transferred to Parkland Junior College in Illinois.

Neil Reed was hampered throughout the season by a dislocated shoulder.

Hodgson, who was being redshirted, left after the first semester.

EVANS COMES THROUGH

Despite some poor performances, 6-8 junior Brian Evans put up the best numbers of his career: 17.4 points, 6.8 rebounds, a team-high 101 assists.

A NEW HAWK Alan Henderson, who led the team in scoring (23.7) and rebounding (9.7), was the 16th overall pick by the Atlanta Hawks. Atlanta Coach Lenny Wilkens said he wanted Henderson because "He can post up,

Alan Henderson finished his career at Indiana as the school's all-time leading rebounder.

face the basket. He rebounds and can block shots. We'll work him in slowly, but we feel like we've gotten a good player."

ANOTHER FINE MESS Knight found a new way to generate negative publicity. This time it came in a nationally televised tirade against an NCAA Tournament press conference moderator.

Knight had spent the season on his best behavior, enduring such silly questions as "Will the loss affect the mystique of playing here?" (after Michigan ended IU's 50-game homecourt winning streak) and "Coach, do your kids work on shooting?" (after IU shot just 29 percent in a loss at Michigan) without incident.

But it all unravelled after the 65-60 loss to Missouri in the opening round of the NCAA Tournament. Moderator Rance Pugmire was mistakenly informed Knight would not come to the press conference, a violation of NCAA policy. Pugmire so informed the press.

Later, when Knight did show up, the following exchange occurred:

Knight: "You know, we only have two people who are going to tell you I'm not going to be here. One is our S.I.D and the other is me. Who the hell told you I wasn't going to be here? I would like to know. Do you have any idea who it was?"

Pugmire: "Yeah, I do coach."

Knight: "Who?"

Pugmire: "I will point him out to you in a while."

Bob Knight reluctantly accepted his latest reprimand from the NCAA, but fired back a reprimand of his own.

Knight: "They were from Indiana, right?"

Pugmire: "No, they were…"

Knight: "No, they weren't from Indiana. And you didn't get it from anybody at Indiana, did you?"

Pugmire: "Could we please continue."

Knight: "No, I will handle this the way I want to handle it now that I'm here. You (bleeped) it up to begin with. Now just sit there or leave. I don't give a (bleep) what you do.

"Now, back to the game…"

Three months later, an NCAA committee reprimanded Knight and fined him a record $30,000. The point, apparently, was to ensure there would be no further incidents.

Knight responded by reprimanding the committee:

"I have been reprimanded by the NCAA Tournament Committee, apparently for the use of a word at a press conference in Boise, Idaho, following our game with Missouri. It was a word I felt was appropriate to the situation, but I certainly know while acceptable to many people, it is not acceptable to many others.

"No specifics for the reprimand have ever been given me in written or verbal form other than to say that a situation that occurred in the 1987 NCAA Tournament (Knight was fined $10,000 for banging his first into the scorer's table) was considered.

"This inclusion of something that took place eight years ago at first bothered me. On reconsideration, I not only accept the committee's thinking, but I endorse it. I urge immediate enactment of an eight-year purity plan that would require all members of the tournament committee to be so guilt-free.

"Seven members of the present nine-man committee either represent or have been at schools as the heads of athletic departments when NCAA violations occurred. My purity plan would mean representation on the committee would be only for those schools that have conducted their athletic business for at least the past eight years in conformity with the NCAA's own rule book. I even have a suggested name for the rule: 'the John 8:7 Rule,' which I have slightly paraphrased to read, "Let him who is without sin cast the first reprimand…

"P.S. My humble suggestion would be that the $30,000 fine be used to fund scholarships for underprivileged students rather than be used as expenses for the NCAA Tournament Committee's annual golf meeting, which this summer is at Cape Cod."

MORE TO COME History indicates the Hoosiers will continue to contend for Big Ten and national title honors while Knight continues to find controversy. As Quinn Buckner said while addressing fans during the players' annual summer reunion:

"You have been extremely supportive of the Indiana basketball program. I say to you very humbly, 'Please take a look at and appreciate Coach Bob Knight. You may never see another one like him.' "

Genesis

In the beginning, Indiana basketball was not what is today – not even close. The Hoosiers struggled to win games and were lucky to draw the equivalent to league night at the local bowling alley.

The school was years behind other state programs in starting basketball. Purdue and Butler had played off and on for years before Indiana decided, around the turn of the century, to take up this relatively new indoor game.

Even then, the Hoosiers were far from developing any kind of hysteria. With such a slow start, basketball almost died a premature death.

LIFE SUPPORT Basketball topped Indiana University's endangered list. It had no coach, few fans, poor prospects. Debate was more popular. Badger fights – an illegal gambling activity that pitted the animals in bloody battles to the death – drew bigger crowds.

Facing budget deficits and limited facilities, school officials saw few options. A program that today dominates the university and ranks among the nation's elite was in danger of being dumped in favor of indoor track.

The Indiana Daily Student displayed the following front page headlines on Thursday, Dec. 3, 1903:

University May Have No Basketball Team
Director Horne Says Indiana May Not Send Out a Varsity Five.

The story explained that J.H. Horne, football coach and athletic director, was considering dropping basketball just three years after the school started it.

"It is now certain that Indiana cannot have both an indoor track team and a basketball team this year. Director Horne is seriously considering the matter, but is not yet ready to say what will be done. He will confer with the athletic board before finally deciding.

"The main difficulty is the gymnasium is not large enough for both teams to work at the same time....Neither team is a money maker. Considerable money, it is said, is lost every year on both. With our present athletic indebtedness (football lost $1,543.06, a sizable total in 1903), this fact is being given much consideration.

"Mr. Horne says there is good material for a track team, but good basketball material is scarce. This inclines him to the discontinuance of basketball rather than track. The matter will be decided by the first of next week."

After a series of closed-door debates, practice schedules were adjusted, additional funds found. Horne kept both sports.

Problems remained. Basketball practice wasn't scheduled to start until just a few days before the Jan. 16 season opener against Salem

The nattily attired Hoosiers of 1900-01 were the first team to play basketball at Indiana. The team won only one of five games.

High School. The Daily Student reported "A captain will be elected and he will have charge of the practice. No competent coach can be secured."

The Daily Student ran the following editorial on Jan. 12, 1904:

"Is basketball dying out? This is a question college men are asking themselves at present. Where are the teams like the ones we had in years gone by? Where is the interest that was then taken in the game? For some reason, it has disappeared and the present team is merely the ghost of its ancestor and the interest displayed by the supporters of athletics is so weak that there is scarcely any attendance at games.

"Shall we let it be said that at Indiana we let the old game die from lack of spirit? No, let us arouse ourselves and, imbued with that real old spirit of Indiana, let us support the game, root for the team and show our sister institutions that we are still there with the goods."

More than 90 years later, the "goods" are still around.

EARLY COACHES

Today, Indiana is one of basketball's coaching Meccas. But in the early years, the school struggled to find qualified candidates – or any candidates.

During the Hoosiers' first season of 1900-01, Athletic Director and football coach J.H. Horne was listed as coach. Actually, that job was done by team captain Ernest Strange and fellow player Thomas Records.

Players were listed as coach in the next three seasons – center Phelps Darby in 1902, guard Willis Coval in '03 and '04. Coval, a highly touted football player, was a basketball reserve.

Zora G. Clevenger

Ralph Jones of the Indianapolis YMCA coached the team at the start of the 1904 season, with Coval taking over at the end when Jones could no longer make practices or games.

The coach for the next two seasons is listed as Zora G. Clevenger, Indiana's first football All-American who became athletic director at Kansas State, Missouri and IU. However, Clevenger was more of a chaperon and schedule-maker for the basketball squad. Team captain Earl Tabor did much of the coaching in 1905, captain Chester Harmeson in 1906.

In 1905, school officials brought in Charles Conner, another Indianapolis YMCA player, to help coach. The Daily Student reported he made an immediate impact on shooting form.

"Coach Conner is drilling the team in the use of the over-hand, one-handed throw. This throw is invaluable to a forward in a tight pitch and is very difficult for a guard to block."

COACHING SEARCH Things reached a low point before the start of the 1906-07 season amid rumors IU wouldn't have a basketball coach because of a lack of funds.

James Sheldon, athletic director and football coach, denied the rumors. He said funds were available and a search was underway. In a Daily Student story, Sheldon "assured the men he has his eye on a man who knows his basketball from A to Z."

For a while, that man was Sheldon himself. It wasn't until Jan. 9, 1907, two days after a season-opening win over DePauw, that Charles McGee was hired. McGee, a physical director at the Indianapolis YMCA, only made practices twice a week. Filling in when he wasn't there was team captain James Sanders.

Problems continued the next year. Louis J. Bohnstadt of Indianapolis, a former player at Indianapolis Manual High School and Butler, was hired as coach, but didn't last. Team captain Ed Cook took over.

The revolving door continued with Robert Harris, John Georgen, Oscar Rackle, James Kase, Arthur Powell, Arthur Berndt, Allen Willisford, G.S. Lowman, Dana M. Evans, Edward O. Stiehm, George W. Levis and Leslie Mann. IU had 18 official coaches – and at least five unofficial ones – in its first 24 seasons. Combined record: 182-174. Championships: zero.

Not until Everett Dean took over in 1924 did Indiana find stability and championship success.

BASKETBALL ON THE BRINK

IU's first game, at Butler on Feb. 8, 1901, came 10 years after Dr. James A. Naismith invented the sport while a physical education instructor in Springfield, Mass.

This was basketball on the brink and opponents were hard to find. IU's five games in its first season were against Butler (twice), Purdue (twice) and Wabash. The only win came against Wabash, 26-17.

Other early opponents included Crawfordsville Boys Club,

Shortridge High School, Salem High School, Indianapolis YMCA, New Albany YMCA and Rayen Athletic Club out of Pennsylvania. The YMCA teams beat the Hoosiers: Indianapolis in 1904, New Albany in 1906.

Experienced players were rare. IU's first team had only three players who had played the game before college.

Basketball wasn't an immediate Bloomington hit, although crowds eventually picked up along with enrollment. In 1905, there were 870 students on campus. By 1908, enrollment topped 2,000.

Terminology was different. You didn't make a shot, you "threw in a goal" or "caged the ball" or "hit the ring." Certain flagrant fouls – or excessive fouling – resulted in automatic team points.

Rules sometimes varied. In a 1906 game at West Lafayette, the free throw line was 15 feet from the basket, five feet fewer than what the Hoosiers were used to. The reason – IU followed AAU rules, which stipulated 20 feet. Purdue used intercollegiate guidelines favored by the Big Nine (later Big Ten) Conference.

BLAME THE CEILING A 1903 story in the Indianapolis News said Indiana's 43-9 win over visiting DePauw was caused because "DePauw was said to be handicapped by a gym with a low ceiling that did not allow taller men to play."

A 1905 matchup between Indiana and Purdue was described by the Daily Student as "A rough contest made slow and uninteresting by many delays in repairing goals and time-outs for injuries…"

Sometimes it appeared basketball became confused with another sport. In that same 1905 IU-Purdue game, the Daily Student reported "There was a three-minute stop by a dispute over interpretation of the new three-men-tackling-the-ball rule."

THE FIRST GAME

Purdue was supposed to be IU's first opponent, but the Feb. 2, 1901, game was postponed by a smallpox epidemic in Bloomington. The illness, which caused enforced quarantines and city-wide vaccinations, caused the Hoosiers to miss a week of practice.

On Feb. 8, Indiana faced Butler. Here's how the Indianapolis News previewed the Hoosiers' prospects:

> "Basketball is comparatively new at the State University (IU), as this is the first season an attempt has been made to have a regular varsity team. Coach Horne has been developing a number of promising candidates during the last six weeks and thinks his men will be able to hold their own against any college team in the State. In addition to the regular varsity squad, class teams have been organized, and several of the fraternities have fives."

Butler won 20-17 in a game The News described as "fast" and "hard fought."

> "For enthusiasm and earnest effort, the basketball game yesterday in the YMCA gymnasium between the Indiana and Butler teams surpassed any contest that has been seen here this

season. While not as brilliant as some of the YMCA exhibitions or as fiercely fought in the hit or miss sort of style of the two high school fives, it was a typical college contest – clean, free from intentional roughness and a hard-fought one from beginning to end.

"Butler won, but only after a nerve-racking contest. Superior team work, coupled with an ability to follow the ball and to shake off the Indiana players, gave the Irvington men the victory by a score of 20 to 17.

"Indiana anticipated defeat, and this worked to her disadvantage. This was, however, Indiana's first basketball game on a foreign floor, and the men at times forgot their carefully-drilled team work and completely lost sight of the fundamental principle of basketball to play their opponent, rather than the ball. This more than anything else, was responsible for the defeat of Indiana."

Forward Ernest Strange led the Hoosiers with nine points.

THE RIVALRY BEGINS

The IU-Purdue rivalry opened with the visiting Boilermakers winning 20-15 on March 4, 1901. Here's how The Indianapolis News described it:

"The game was evenly played and was won by Alex Smith's goal throwing. Purdue played a fast game, though several of the men put an undue amount of roughness into it. (Purdue's) Loyd Lucas was ruled out on this account. The Indiana men did not play their opponents close enough and (Ernest) Strange lost his opportunity to win by missing twelve chances at goal. (Phelps) Darby and (Alvah) Rucker each played a strong game for Indiana, while (J.F.G.) Miller showed up best for Purdue."

LONE VICTORY Indiana's only win of that debut season came by a 26-17 score against Wabash. The game was, according to The Indianapolis News, "characterized by much erratic playing. Indiana showed marked improvement. Strange and Rucker played the strongest game. Loop, who played center for Wabash, did the best individual work for his team, while Captain Wright and Adams were in the game at all times."

STATE TITLE At that time, there were no conference or national titles to shoot for. There was, however, a state championship, which went to the team that compiled the best record against Indiana schools.

Purdue and Butler decided to play for the state title in 1901 because both had beaten Indiana. While neither had played Hanover, officials from both schools agreed Hanover was not very good (Hanover's opinion wasn't considered). Purdue beat Butler 41-12 to finish undefeated.

THE SECOND SEASON

IU's first practice of its second season came on Jan. 9, 1901, six days before the season-opener against Butler. Eleven players were selected from their performances in physical education classes, intramural games and a 50-man open tryout. A story in the Indiana Daily Student described that first practice:

> "The men are still weak in both passing and throwing goals (shooting) from the field. The varsity scored almost at will while the reserves were content with one field goal and two (free throws). Individually, the team is strong and with practice to develop team play, should make it interesting for any team in the state."

Not interesting enough. Butler won 17-15. The Hoosiers finished 4-4.

BAD DEFEAT Indiana's 71-25 loss to Purdue on March 7, 1902, remains the second-worst loss ever to the Boilermakers, topped only by a 62-15 game in 1910. The Hoosiers trailed 41-5 at halftime.

The 1902 Boilermakers were inspired by the death of guard Harold Cook, who died a few days before the IU game after contracting a severe cold following a game with Butler.

THE STRUGGLES CONTINUE

The Hoosiers opened the 1903-04 season against Salem High School, described in newspaper reports as "one of the best teams in southern Indiana." IU won 60-18.

Consecutive road losses to DePauw (38-28) and Rose Poly (23-18) followed. Newspaper accounts attributed them to "basket settings and arrangement of posts," although team captain Leslie Maxwell offered a more knowledgeable explanation.

"The playing of the team was erratic and showed some practice is yet needed....The men did not seem to go in with the determination and vim to win....The main thing we need is more confidence, better team work and a sure foul-goal scorer."

The Hoosiers also needed a coach.

"The material is good, probably the best Indiana has ever had, but they need someone to instruct them on the minor points of the game," said Athletic Director J.H. Horne.

"An effort is being made to secure a coach. It is probable that some person from Indianapolis will be secured..."

That person was M.L. Pritchard, described as "an experienced basketball coach" and an "old Indianapolis YMCA star." At the time, YMCAs across the country had the best, most-experienced players.

Pritchard, a disciplinarian who stressed conditioning, was a part-time coach. He only traveled to Bloomington for games and practices the day before games. When he wasn't around, Maxwell filled in.

BEAT THE BOILERS Pritchard was brought in specifically to beat Purdue, which was 6-0 against the Hoosiers. After victories over DePauw (33-23) and Wabash (32-25), Pritchard talked equal to the task.

"I can't see how Purdue can win when her showings against (Wabash and DePauw) were not as good as Indiana's," he told the Daily Student. "Yet, I see dispatches from the Purdue camp that they are claiming an easy victory over us. I cannot understand their methods of figuring."

Pritchard's understanding wasn't helped when Purdue dominated the second half in a 31-18 victory.

The Daily Student described it this way:

"It was a case of being outclassed, but the determination which Indiana displayed and the gameness with which the team clung to the last chance of victory, like a small animal in the clutches of a larger adversary, won the admiration of the supporters."

But not necessarily the admiration of the unnamed writer.

"At no time in the second half did the local team display any characteristics of winners."

IN THE HUNT At 4-3, IU was one game behind first-place Purdue in the state standings entering the teams' rematch and season-finale in West Lafayette. A Hoosier victory would cause a tie and require a third game to decide the champion.

Purdue was hindered by injuries to three starters. IU, coming off 50-19 victories over Wabash and Rose Poly, once again expected a victory.

But the Hoosiers, who couldn't practice in days leading up to the game because their gymnasium was being used by a convention, lost again. After a 12-12 halftime tie, Purdue won 22-21 in front of a crowd of 550. Chester Harmeson led IU with eight points.

The next season, the Hoosiers started Big Ten play. It would be 22 years, with the arrival of Everett Dean, before IU would win a championship. Beating Purdue would come much sooner.

HOW CREAM 'N CRIMSON BECAME INDIANA'S COLORS

Ever wonder how Cream 'n Crimson came to be Indiana's school colors? Here's one version according to an unidentified alumnus in a Nov. 13, 1903, Daily Student story:

"When I was a senior in 1888, our class conceived the idea of publishing a volume which would reflect life and affairs at the university. No previous class had attempted anything of this nature, but that did not daunt us in the least.

"After quite an amount of discussion, we decided to issue a Commencement number of The Student (a university publication), which was then published monthly and illustrate it with pictures of the various fraternities and college organizations.

"The next question that confronted us was the colors to be used in decorating the binding of the volume. Before that time, there had been no official University colors, so the class of '88, 39 in number, met to decide what Indiana's future colors should be. The Cream and Crimson were chosen without a dissenting vote and, with the appearance of the Commencement number of The Student, they made their formal debut."

BOILERMAKERS GO DOWN

The Feb. 20, 1905, headline screamed from the front page:

INDIANA DEFEATS THE BOILERMAKERS

In the Most Exciting Game Ever Seen Here, Varsity Basketball Five Humiliates Old Purdue By a Score of 29 to 14.

After five years and nine games of futility, including a 38-20 set-back a month earlier in West Lafayette, the Hoosiers had finally beaten the Boilermakers behind forward Chester Harmeson's 16 points.

Purdue, which started basketball in 1896, was a Midwest power. By 1905, the Boilermakers had won five consecutive state titles. IU's victory ended Purdue's chance to make it six (Wabash won it).

Here is how the Daily Student described it:

> "Indiana won the prettiest game of the year Saturday night from the much-vaunted wearers of the old gold and black. 'Purdue!' was the war-cry and Purdue bit the dust before the nervy wearers of the cream and crimson.

> "Everyone was excited, everyone rooted, everyone called upon favorite deities, pulling for Indiana and the way in which the crimson-clad men responded made the oldest inhabitant leap upon his chair and shout 'Bully for Indiana.'.... No Indiana team ever put up a better fight from whistle to whistle."

SORE LOSERS After losing to Indiana in consecutive seasons in 1905 and '06, Purdue dropped the Hoosiers for the 1906-07 season. IU was replaced by Rose Poly of Terre Haute. The series resumed the following season.

BIASED TIMES

Unbiased reporting – and, perhaps, unbiased officiating – had not yet evolved. Here is the Daily Student's account of New Albany YMCA's 18-17 victory over visiting IU on Feb. 27, 1906:

> "Everybody unites in agreeing that the work of the official who reigned with a tyrannical hand was the vilest and most unfair ever perpetrated. On three different occasions, fouls were called on (Clifford) Woody just as he had thrown the ball in the basket for a field goal, and no possible motive for the umpire verdicts could be found except his desire to give the visitors the short end of it. Despite the handicap, the Crimson athletes showed wonderful tenacity and were in the van at many stages."

An account from a 1905 loss to Rose Poly of Terre Haute stated "Referee Atridge was very strict and insisted on several rulings not familiar to the Cream and Crimson men."

Objectivity hit a major bump when IU team captain and forward E.R. Taber wrote the Daily Student story following the Hoosiers' 38-20 loss to Purdue in 1905.

> "The work of the officials was wretched. Many times when

the Indiana forwards were throwing at the goal, they were knocked over or straight-armed, and instead of awarding a point to Indiana and a chance at foul goal, the ball was thrown up between players."

Taber's criticism may have been justified. One of the officials was a Purdue student named McNally.

BIZARRE FINISH

A funny thing happened to Indiana during its 24-23 victory at Cincinnati on March 1, 1906 – it lost 26-23 in overtime.

Regulation ended in confusion. The IU scorer had the Hoosiers winning 24-23. The official scorer had it 23-23. After some discussion, the referee announced Indiana had won. The crowd left; the players went to the locker rooms.

Meanwhile, the Indiana scorekeeper discovered he had made a mistake. The score was 23-23. He notified officials, who called back the players, "some of whom were taking their baths," for an overtime period. Cincinnati scored three times in the six-minute extra session for the victory.

That was part of a five-game tailspin that cost the Hoosiers a winning record (they finished 7-9) and spoiled the early season prediction of Butler Coach Wingard, who stated after IU whipped his team 42-11 that "Indiana will win the state championship in a walk."

RECORD-BREAKING SCORER On Jan. 27, 1906, forward Chester Harmeson scored a school-record 28 points in a 46-21 victory over the New Albany YMCA. He had 11 field goals and six free throws.

To put Harmeson's achievement in perspective in such a low-scoring era, it wasn't until March 4, 1938, that Ernie Andres broke it with a 30-point performance in a 45-35 win over Illinois.

THE 1907-11 PERIOD

Indiana went 30-28 during this span. In 1907, team captains Ed Cook and Harlan McCoy were called "the speediest pair of forwards in the state" by the Daily Student.

In 1908, Clifford Woody burned Rose Poly for 20 points in a 30-11 victory. It was a year before another Hoosier scored 20. That was Dean Barnhart, who got 21 against DePauw. Two years later, he scored 21 against Rose Poly and 25 against DePauw, becoming the first IU player to score at least 20 points twice in a season.

Ten years passed before another Hoosier reached the 20-point mark. Everett Dean scored 21 in a 33-11 victory over Ohio State on Feb. 14, 1921.

LEAN YEARS

The low point of the early years came from 1911-15. The Hoosiers were 17-43 overall, 3-39 in the Big Ten.

The coach for two of those seasons was Arthur "Cotton" Berndt, a former IU standout who had lettered in football, basketball and baseball by the time he'd graduated in 1910. He also served as Indiana's athletic director and baseball coach.

How bad was IU? In December of 1913, it lost a "vacation game" (exhibition) to the Detch Specials out of Indianapolis by a 48-5 score. That led to the following Daily Student preview before the season opener at Illinois:

"Although prospects are none too bright, Coach Berndt is holding out all kinds of hope his men will show something against Illinois."

It didn't happen. The Hoosiers lost 35-6, then followed with a 59-15 loss to Wisconsin.

LOOKING GOOD For the first time in five years, the Hoosiers got new uniforms. The Daily Student described them as having "A natty appearance. A white jersey with Indiana across the front, grey pants and maroon socks."

PLAYING BAD As the losses mounted – five in January, six in February – the tone of Daily Student articles became more caustic.

"Indiana's basketball team should make a good cast for Firefly (a popular play at the time). How they do love that hit song, 'Sympathy' " the paper wrote in a Jan. 27 article. A Feb. 23 story stated, "You never hear of an (Indiana player) being kicked off for professionalism because we never have them fast enough to break into that select company."

TIME TO CELEBRATE

The disappointment of Indiana's 2-12 record (1-11 in the Big Ten) in the 1913-14 season was eased by a 30-28 victory over Purdue. A late free throw by IU's James Frenzel sent the game into overtime. Bobby Maxwell and Russell Kirkpatrick scored in the extra session to give the Hoosiers their first victory over Purdue in seven years.

That win caused a celebration that was only partly muted by the city's new alcohol prohibition laws designed to make Bloomington a "model city morally." Here's how the Daily Student reported it in its March 4 edition:

Indiana Downs Purdue In Overtime Game, The Jinx Is Dead
Crimson Win First Conference Game in Two Years, First Defeat of Purdue on Local Floor in History.

"Indiana, with the jinx dead and buried, went in last night and defeated Purdue in perhaps the greatest game of basketball ever played on the local floor by a score of 30- 28. A five-minute overtime period was needed to determine the winner, the two teams having scored 26 points when the whistle blew ending the regulation game.

"What a shame it was that the town is dry and the blind tiger (saloon) owners all locked up in the cooler (jail)....It was a game of do or die and what a relief to see Purdue take the part of the died."

EARLY ARENAS

It was January, 1914, and controversy raged. Students gathered petitions. Alumni demanded change. Alarmed school officials huddled behind closed doors.

The solution, everyone agreed, was obvious. Assembly Hall had to go.

The one-story, wooden frame structure – where teams practiced and played, and students attended physical education classes – had become a breeding ground for disease.

GYMNASIUM – MENACE TO STUDENT'S HEALTH blared a Daily Student headline. For a month, the paper put a photo of the facility on its front page as part of its campaign to build a new gymnasium. The impetus came with a Jan. 27 story quoting an unidentified school official:

"After a thorough investigation of general hygienic conditions and especially the cases of disease alleged to have been contracted in or around the gymnasium of Indiana University, we believe the sanitary conditions are such as to permanently render it a positive menace to student health...many cases of gym itch, blood poison, boils and other diseases so prevalent this winter and alleged to have been caused by infection around the gymnasium."

Not just IU students were affected. The gym was also the site of the state high school basketball tournament.

University officials urged the construction of a new gym. The old facility – located near the Union Building – had been built in 1895 at a

MOVING ON After a follow-up season of 4-9, Berndt had enough. He left to become the head of the welfare department for Showers Brothers Furniture Company in Bloomington.

IU was an unofficial training camp for Showers. In 1922, less than a month before the start of the season, Coach George Levis resigned to accept a Showers' management position.

THE 1916-20 PERIOD

Indiana opened 8-0 in the 1916-17 season and 7-0 the following year.

The Indiana team of 1917-18 with Coach Dana Evans.

cost of $12,000. It seated only 600 and lacked adequate facilities.

A new 2,000-seat gym – similar to one Purdue had built six years earlier for $100,000 – would cost around $200,00.

In 1916, IU got a new gym, relegating the older facility to use as a theater for plays and performances. It was also the setting for speeches by such notables as Presidents William Howard Taft and Teddy Roosevelt, and perennial presidential contender William Jennings Bryan. It was razed in 1938.

The original Assembly Hall (1895-1938).

The 13-6 mark posted in 1916-17 set a school record for most victories.

Dana Evans, who coached from 1917-19, became the first IU coach to get 20 victories. His two-year record was 20-11.

When a new coach couldn't be found the following season, football coach Edward Stiehm took over even though he knew almost nothing about the sport. The reason – he needed the money. However, with Everett Dean at center and the players doing the actual coaching, the Hoosiers went 13-8 to tie the school record for victories.

CONTENDERS AT LAST

The 1920-21 Hoosiers had the city buzzing. They had three returning starters from the previous season's 13-8 team. That included Dean, poised to become IU's first All-American. The Hoosiers also had a new, offensive-minded coach in George Levis, who arrived in Bloomington after several successful seasons at Carleton College in Minnesota.

Indiana started 5-0 and scored at least 34 points in every game, impressive for the era. After whipping the Evansville YMCA 44-15, Dean leading the way with 14 points, the Daily Student reported that "Coach George Levis' offensive basketball machine again failed to find a foeman worthy of its steel in the touted Evansville YMCA here last night. The visitors' defense had much the aspect of a sieve."

The Hoosier found a worthy foeman two weeks later in Merchants H & L out of Indianapolis, losing 34-21. According to the

The 1920 Hoosier team. First Row, left to right: Edward H. DeHority, Edward C. Von Tress, Herman E. Schuler, Captain Everett S. Dean, William H. Dobbins, Mr. Cox, Relle T. Aldridge, Kermit R. Maynard. Second Row: Mr. Colpitts, trainer; Robert C. Marxson, Eugene S. Thomas, Lawrence M. Busby, Russell D. Hauss, Glenn A. Johnson, Coach George Levis.

Daily Student, "Johnson, the lanky Merchants forward, was responsible for the defeat of the Crimson five. He scored six field goals and 10 foul goals, for a total of 22 points."

Indiana then won six straight and moved atop the Big Ten standings with a 3-0 record. A 31-10 win over visiting Northwestern – the Hoosiers ended the game with a 14-1 run – received this Daily Student write-up:

"Uncorking a scoring spree such has never been seen in Indiana University's new gymnasium, Coach Levis' Crimson net combination swept Northwestern's heavy team off its feet in the last six minutes of play as it won its third straight Conference game."

The game drew more than 1,000. Leaving nothing to chance, IU officials scheduled a pre-game boxing exhibition in the gymnasium to help spur attendance.

SUCCESS HAS ITS PRICE Mounting victories produced bigger crowds and rising prices. A ticket cost 50 cents at the start of the season, 75 cents at the end.

YA GOTTA BELIEVE Not even a 27-18 loss at Purdue could spoil the enthusiasm, as a Feb. 2 Daily Student story reported.

" 'We will win the conference' and 'Beat Purdue' are circulating throughout the campus, among alumni and over the state in general. Going down to a smarting defeat at the hands of Purdue, in a game in which the crippled Indiana team (guard Bobby Marxson played with a torn arm ligament) did all but win, has only brought about a greater spirit and a greater determination among the players, the coaches and all Indiana fans."

UNCHARTED TERRITORY In late February the Hoosiers, who had never finished better than fourth in the conference, were first with a 6-1 league record. This irritated Hall of Fame football coach Amos Alonzo Stagg, who also guided the Chicago basketball team (Chicago was then a Big Ten member). Stagg said the Hoosiers were benefiting from "an easy schedule."

Stagg may have had a point. A week later, Indiana's season crashed against Iowa. The Hawkeyes beat the Hoosiers twice in six days to start a four-game slide that dropped IU to sixth. ·

LAST CHANCE Indiana still had a shot at the league championship by beating Purdue in Bloomington in the season's next-to-the-last game. Daily Student accounts stated Hoosier fans were primed.

"Armed with castoff tin-ware, sardine cans, second-hand automobiles, dish pans and worn out alarm clocks, the he-men of the student body will gather to make the Boilermakers feel at home. 'We want noise rather than ammunition,' said Eddie Brackett the organizer. 'If every tin can rooter will keep up the pep the entire game, I guarantee we will trim Purdue.' "

The story said a section on the west end of the gym was reserved for "men who bring metal ware to the game."

More than 1,200 spectators and 2,500 tin cans filled the gym. It wasn't enough. Purdue won 28-20 to end the Hoosiers' title hopes.

HARD TIMES Even with a successful team in the 1920-21 season, IU struggled financially. Part of the reason was too many free passes to games, as related in a March 1 Daily Student story.

"The number of passes heretofore granted for athletic contests has been enormous. In many cases, the passes used at games equaled almost 50 percent of the total number attending.

"Due to this fact, and because the athletic department has never broken even in financial matters, (Athletic Director) E.O. Stiehm, Bursar U.H. Smith and other University authorities are very closely probing the matter."

The story said that of the 610 fans who attended the Indiana-Louisville game, 152 had complimentary tickets and 301 had season coupons. That left 157 paid admissions.

THE 1922-23 SEASON

Another hot start fizzled with a season-ending three-game losing streak for an 8-7 record, 5-7 in the Big Ten, under first-year coach Leslie Mann.

Still, there was reason for optimism. Forward Mike Nyikos, a 6-foot sophomore who didn't become eligible until January because of grades, became IU's second All-Big Ten player (Dean was first). Despite missing two games, Nyikos ranked fifth in the conference with 93 points.

He was almost unstoppable in a 23-21 victory over conference-leader and previously unbeaten Iowa. Here's how the Daily Student described it:

TEAM RULES

Here were the 1922-23 team rules: 1) Include no eating between meals; 2) No eating candy, no drinking of cocoa cola or soft drinks; 3) No smoking or use of tobacco in any form; 4) No drinking of coffee or alcohol in any form; 5) In bed by 10:30 p.m; And finally, "The player who cheats, sneaks around and breaks training is a traitor. He is a man without honor or respect. He would falter in the pinch for Indiana and ought to be, and will be, dealt with accordingly."

"Rushing Iowa with a terrific offense built chiefly around Nyikos, Indiana tonight accomplished what no other team has been able to do this year and downed the Hawkeyes 23-21 in the most thrilling and 'dope' upsetting game of the season.

"The game was from start to finish a case of too much Nyikos. The Indiana forward was stationed directly under the Hawkeye basket and by a clever system of feeding the ball to him, enabled him to cage five field goals to which he added 11 free throws for a total of 21 of Indiana's 23 points."

THE 1923-24 SEASON

Despite losing three games by two points or less, IU finished 11-6 and 7-5. The Hoosiers won seven of their last nine games.

In early December, a few days before the season opener against Terre Haute Normal, Coach Leslie Mann ordered all practices behind locked doors.

"This will prevent any information as to the style of play used by the Indiana quintet from seeping out to opposing teams," the coach said in Dec. 4, 1923 Daily Student story.

After the 27-24 victory, a testy Mann said "If players are going to think of the number of points they can score rather than of playing team work, they have no place on my team."

UNWANTED BREAK In February, the team got five days off "when the baskets were taken down so that a musical could be held in the Gym." It came during the middle of a five-game win streak.

NYIKOS IS GONE On Feb. 8, Mike Nyikos withdrew from school after flunking out. At the time, he was the Big Ten's leading scorer with 64 points in seven games. He enrolled at Notre Dame, but was later declared permanently ineligible.

Indiana still won four of its last six games thanks to forward Harlan Logan, described by team manager W. Earl Keisker as "slim and frail in body, but very clever on the floor and exceedingly fast."

Forward Mike Nyikos played very well for the Hoosiers but had trouble in school.

The Everett Dean Years

Everett Dean jolted Indiana from its nearly quarter-century of mediocrity. During his tenure as a player and coach, the Hoosiers became perennial Big Ten challengers, winning titles in 1926, '28 and 36, and placing second two other times. Before his 1917 arrival, IU's best finish had been third in 1906, when there were only seven league teams.

As a player, the 6-foot center was IU's first All-American, averaging 10.7 points as a senior in 1921. Here's how the Daily Student described him:

> "He is the man around whom the whole play of the Crimson varsity revolves. His size, speed, basket eye and head work make him an invaluable scorer in that remarkable offense which Coach Levis has developed. His early season work makes him loom as All-Conference material."

With Dean in the lineup, the Hoosiers were 10-7 in 1919, 13-8 in 1920 and 15-6 in 1921. As a senior, Dean scored 21 points against Ohio State, the first IU player to reach 20 points since Dean Barnhart got 21 against Rose Poly in 1911.

Dean took his studies seriously. As a senior, he won the Big Ten medal of honor for academic and athletic excellence.

Not bad for someone who was never recruited by IU. Dean's father, William, talked Coach Dana Evans into taking his son. William Dean told Evans his son was pretty good and since he was going to IU anyway, they'd appreciate it if the coach would let him try out.

Evans did.

FORGET CONNIE MACK After graduating in 1921, Dean was offered a pro baseball contract by Hall of Fame manager Connie Mack. However, Mack soon took back the offer and Dean went on to coach basketball and baseball for four seasons at Carleton College in Northfield, Minn. He was recommended for the job by IU Coach George Levis, who had coached there before coming to Bloomington.

Indiana Coach Everett Dean

Dean's Carleton basketball teams compiled a record of 48-4 with three straight conference championships.

When he took the Indiana job in 1924 at age 26, IU's enrollment was 3,000. There were no scholarships and recruiting was done through coach and alumni contacts. Every conference team played man-to-man defense because the league coaches had a "gentlemen's" agreement not to play zone.

QUICK SUCCESS Dean's disciplined, methodical, work-for-good-shots style made an immediate impact. His first team went 12-5 and was the Big Ten runner-up. His second team went 12-5 and tied Purdue, Michigan and Iowa for the conference championship. All had 8-4 marks. It was the Hoosiers' first Big Ten title.

Dean's 12-year record in Bloomington was 162-93, 96-72 in Big Ten play.

He coached four All-Americans: Branch McCracken in 1930, Vernon Huffman in 1936, Ken Gunning in 1937 and Ernie Andres in 1938.

"He was a very, very fine man and coach," Huffman told Inside Indiana years later. "I was always impressed with the way he coached and handled his players. He was an excellent teacher and a real gentleman. I don't think anyone can say enough good things about the man."

RECRUITING MCCRACKEN Dean's recruitment of McCracken is the stuff of legends. According to one story, the coach was in Monrovia, Ind., and saw this strapping lad knee deep in a swollen stream, catching floating watermelons washed away by an upstream flash flood. Dean convinced him to come to Bloomington and told him to pick up his friend John Wooden, an all-state guard from Martinsville, on his way to campus. When McCracken arrived at Wooden's house, Wooden was gone. Purdue Coach Ward Lambert had taken him to West Lafayette the night before. Wooden went on to become a three-time All-American for the Boilermakers and a Hall of Fame coach at UCLA.

BESTING LAMBERT Bob Dro, who played on IU's 1940 NCAA championship team, related his recruitment.

"(Dean) recruited me and it was quite a deal back then," said Dro, who was from tiny Berne, Ind. "I had told him I was going to IU and then I was visited by Purdue Coach Piggy Lambert. Lambert offered what I thought was a better deal and I wrote Coach Dean and told him I was going to Purdue.

"Well, he called me and asked that we talk before I made a final decision. My dad and I drove to the Washington Hotel in Indianapolis to meet with him. He won me over and I left with him for Bloomington."

MR. VERSATILE Dean also coached the Indiana baseball team to three Big Ten championships and a record of 186-93. One of his pitchers, Whitey Wilshire, still holds the school earned run record (1.12 in 1934).

LEAVING INDIANA In the summer of 1938, Dean left IU for Stanford. The decision, he later said, wasn't easy.

"The university was looking for a Midwesterner and they preferred someone from Indiana," he said in a Feb. 28, 1981, IU basketball program story. "My wife (Lena) and I had talked about possible moves. We both liked the area and admired Stanford. It, like Indiana, rated among the best. It was the only place we would ever have moved to."

In the spring of 1940, using the freshmen Dean had recruited, McCracken coached the Hoosiers to the NCAA championship.

In 1942, Dean guided Stanford to the national title in his only NCAA Tournament appearance. With a 3-0 record, he remains the only coach with a perfect NCAA Tournament mark.

After that season, he wrote "Progressive Basketball," which related his philosophy on coaching.

CLOSING IT OUT Dean coached at Stanford until 1955. His basketball record was 167-120, including 28-4 in that national championship season. His five-year baseball record was 125-82-4 and included a berth in the 1953 College World Series.

Because of a mild heart condition, Dean gave up basketball in 1950. He retired in 1955 to his home town of Salem, Ind., where he built a home, farmed and became involved in community affairs.

He was inducted into the Helms Hall of Fame in 1958, the Indiana Hall of Fame in '65, the Naismith Memorial Basketball Hall of Fame in '66 and the American Association of Coaches Hall of Fame in '76. He was also a member of the initial IU Athletic Hall of Fame class in 1982.

Dean stayed close to IU officials after his retirement. He became friends with Bob Knight, who often sought Dean's advice.

"Basketball has lost its finest gentleman, its finest coach," Knight said after Dean's death in 1993 at the age of 95. "There has never been a coach who was Everett's equal in ethics or honesty. If a Hall of Fame were ever established for true gentlemen in athletics, Everett would be its first inductee.

"If there has ever been a finer man than Everett Dean, God kept him for His own friend."

After retirement, Everett and Lena Dean attend a game in the new Assembly Hall.

Everett Dean (back row, second from left) coached the 1924-25 Hoosiers to a 12-5 record.

THE 1924-25 SEASON

At 6-7, center Paul Parker was IU's tallest player ... Dean had 45 players try out in October. The squad was cut to 30 by early November, to 16 two weeks later. School was dismissed for 10 days in late January because of a water shortage. The team, in the middle of a seven-game winning streak, remained on campus to practice ... IU's 51-33 victory over Michigan was the most points any Big Ten team would score that season ... The Hoosiers expenses for seven road games: $1,721. After the 12-5, conference-runner-up season, a Daily Student story had this to say about the new coach: "Everett Dean, Indiana's basketball coach,...has caused the Crimson to be feared in Big Ten basketball circles."

INDIANA-KENTUCKY DEBUT On Dec. 18, 1924, Indiana beat Kentucky in Lexington, 20-18, in the first game of what has became a fierce rivalry. IU led the series 20-18 through the 1994-95 season.

THE 1925-26 SEASON – THE FIRST TITLE

With four starters returning, expectations were high. The hole was at center, but the Hoosiers found a potential star in football standout Frank Sibley.

After a mid-season slump, IU won its last five games, including three on the road, to win a share of its first Big Ten championship. The Hoosiers finished 12-5 overall, 8-4 in the conference.

More than 40 players tried out. Dean kept preseason practices entertaining by ending them with volleyball games. Handball was used for conditioning.

Indiana opened with a 47-26 home victory over Miami of Ohio before a packed Men's Gymnasium crowd of 3,000. The price of a ticket – $1.25.

After a 33-20 loss at DePauw, the Hoosiers rebounded with victories over Wabash (35-27), Kentucky (34-23) and Minnesota (33-28).

Against Kentucky, Sibley came off the bench to score a game-high 12 points. Beating Minnesota gave IU its first Big Ten-opening victory in five seasons.

BRIEF SLUMP Wisconsin stayed undefeated in conference play by edging the Hoosiers 33-31 in mid-January despite IU forward Julius Krueger's 14 points. Guard Jack Winston, Indiana's best leaper, jumped center.

Indiana lost its second straight game as host Iowa posted a 29-22 victory. The Hawkeyes' tight defense limited Krueger to just five points. Iowa guard Harold Miller went 2-for-18 from the field for six points.

BOUNCING BACK The Hoosiers rebounded with a 39-31 victory at Northwestern. Sibley led the way with 12 points. However, according to an Indianapolis Star story, the real key was the 6-3 Winston, "the giant who jumped at center and then retired to play back guard...His (defense) made Purple short shots almost impossible."

IU added a 37-34 victory over Purdue and a 30-20 win over Iowa to move into second place in the league standings behind Wisconsin.

MOMENTUM ENDS The Boilermakers slowed the Hoosiers with a 31-29 victory. With the score tied at 29 in the final minute, reserve guard Robert Wilson drove the length of the court for a layup. IU's Arthur Beckner missed a tip-in at the buzzer that would have sent the game into overtime. Beckner led Indiana with 19 points.

HEARTBREAKER The Hoosiers lost its offense in a 21-20 loss to Illinois. That dropped IU to 4-4 in Big Ten play, two games behind co-leaders Wisconsin and Illinois.

With seven minutes left and leading 21-18, the Illini went to a stall. IU got a basket from Robert Correll, but Krueger and Winston missed long attempts that would have won it.

WINNING OUT The Hoosiers didn't lose another game, beating Minnesota (41-23), Carleton (38-36), Northwestern (34-28), Illinois

The Indiana squad of 1925-26 claimed the school's first Big Ten Championship, finishing with a 12-5 record, 8-4 in conference play.

(28-25) and Wisconsin (35-20). The Hoosiers rallied from a 13-point deficit against Carleton.

CLINCHING THE TITLE The Wisconsin victory enabled IU to share the crown with Purdue and Michigan. Here's how The Indianapolis Star reported it:

> "Krueger, Beckner, Sibley, Sponsler and Winston out-played, out-fought and out-shot Wisconsin at the Men's Gymnasium last night, and as a result, Coach Everett Dean's flying five went into a tie with Purdue and Michigan for its first conference basketball championship."

The victory was especially significant for Dean, who lost a shot at a championship his senior year when the Hoosiers folded down the stretch.

"The Indiana team gave one of the best exhibitions of fight and determination ever shown by any team," he said. "They fought for 40 minutes and as a unit. Every man deserves much praise for coming through in a real pinch. The exhibition of fight and determination shown against Wisconsin should be a mark for future Indiana basketball teams to shoot at."

SCORING CHAMP Beckner's 15 points in the season finale against Wisconsin gave him a conference-leading 108, one more than Purdue's George Spradling. Beckner (who would go on to coach Muncie Central to the 1951 high school state championship) was the first of IU's five Big Ten scoring champions. The others were Branch McCracken in 1930, Don Schlundt from 1953-55, Archie Dees in 1957 and '58, George McGinnis in 1971.

"There is some dispute among authorities about the exact total of Beckner, but the Indiana book is official," wrote the Daily Student.

Beckner's scoring was held down by the fact basketballs back then were laced and uneven, and a player fouled out after four fouls.

LONG AND SHORT Statistics were kept on "short" and "long" shots. Although specific distance weren't listed, any shot from inside the foul lane was generally considered short....The Hoosiers never shot better than 25 percent from the field and finished with a team average of 22 percent.

ALL-BIG TEN Julius Krueger made the first team, with Beckner on the second.

Said Dean: "There was no better shooter in the conference than Krueger. He had amazing speed for his dribble and was a master controller of the ball. Beckner was a rough and tumble floor man, a ball hawk who was always in the middle of the melee. He recovered more loose balls than any man in the conference."

THE 1926-27 SEASON

Indiana came back for an even better year – 13-4 record, 9-3 in the Big Ten. However, Michigan won the title with a 10-2 mark.

The Hoosiers won their first seven games before Michigan – overcoming an early 8-0 deficit – beat them 31-27. That started a month-long stretch of win-one, lose-one play.

However, Indiana beat Michigan in the rematch, 37-34, and ended the season with three straight victories.

Beckner and Krueger again led the Hoosiers. Beckner had 130 points to Krueger's 119. Beckner was a second-team All-Big Ten selection. Krueger made the third team.

THE 1927-28 SEASON –
ANOTHER CO-CHAMPIONSHIP

The Hoosiers' 15-2 record (.882) set a school mark for winning percentage. They went 10-2 in the conference. Both losses came on the road: Michigan (42-41) and Purdue (28-25).

IU shared the Big Ten title with Purdue, which also went 15-2 and 10-2.

The Hoosiers managed this despite the graduation of Krueger, Sibley and Winston. Beckner returned, but only for the first semester before he graduated. He was replaced by James Strickland, who finished in the top 10 in conference scoring.

MCCRACKEN ARRIVES The Hoosiers were boosted by sophomore center Branch McCracken, in his first varsity year (freshmen were ineligible). Here's how the Daily Student described him:

> "Height, ranginess and cleverness, the three attributes of a good center, are so manifest in Branch McCracken that he already is one of the leading members of the squad….He has all the natural attributes of a good netman, coach Dean believes, and is expected to bear watching in spite of his experience."

FREE THROW TOURNEY To add interest and improve shooting, Dean decided to hold a season-long tourney from early November through

With the arrival of sophomore Branch McCracken (front row, center), the Hoosiers and Coach Everett Dean (back row, behind McCracken) tied Purdue for the conference title.

December. Seven of 15 players made at least 75 percent of their attempts.

IT'S A SECRET Not wanting word of IU's prospects getting out, Dean held numerous closed-door practices.

PLAY BALL Indiana easily won its first five games, with only Franklin staying within 10 points. McCracken scored eight points in the opener over Franklin, then followed with efforts of 16, 14 and 24 points.

MICHIGAN WINS The Wolverines overcame a Hoosier stall to rally for their 42-41 victory. Here's how the Michigan Daily described it:
Wolverine Closing Rally Upsets Indiana, 42-41 – Fast Hoosier Five Victims of Desperate Maize and Blue Attack In Closing Moments.

"Thrilling a monster crowd beyond description, Michigan's battling Wolverines tore through a furious game that was more than basketball to annex their first Western Conference victory at the expense of a fast-breaking Indiana five in a whirlwind finish."

Later, with IU leading 36-31 and trying to stall, Michigan rallied. Michigan took a 42-39 lead. McCracken scored to pull the Hoosiers within a point, but the Hoosiers couldn't regain possession.
Beckner led IU with 13 points.

BOUNCING BACK The Hoosiers followed with routs of Chicago and Illinois, outscoring them by a combined score of 79-41. McCracken had 29 of the points.

PURDUE STRIKES AGAIN Indiana took early leads of 6-0 and 9-4 before Purdue rallied for a three-point victory. The Boilermakers led by nine with two minutes left before Strickland – in because McCracken had fouled out – made three long baskets to pull the Hoosiers within three. They never got any closer.

"The entire contest was marked by long shots and close guarding, verging on roughness because of the intense rivalry," wrote sports editor Robert Wagner in the Purdue Exponent …"It established the Boilermaker quintet a little more firmly in the Big Ten upper berth."

But not for long. Indiana won its final eight games – including revenge victories over Purdue (40-37) and Michigan (36-34) to join the Boilermakers at the top.

BOILERMAKERS GO DOWN IU handed Purdue its first loss of the season, building a 40-23 lead and then holding on.

Shooting was poor: the Boilermakers were 16-for-74 from the field; IU was 13-for-62. The key came at the free throw line – Indiana was 14-for-17 to Purdue's 7-for-15.

McCracken scored 11 points despite an early injury when Purdue's Babe Wheeler "took his feet out from under him as he tried to jump for a basket," wrote the Indianapolis News.

"McCracken, the boy who led the fight for the Hoosiers after being pretty badly injured early in the game, was the only player put out by personals, but this was too late to be of any benefit to Purdue."

BACK IN FRONT The two-point win over Michigan pushed the Hoosiers into first place. McCracken scored 14 points to take over the Big Ten scoring lead.

Two days later, IU ended its season with a 27-23 victory over Illinois.

McCracken totaled 173 total points in 17 games, for a 10.1 average.

Michigan's Benny Oosterbaan finished as the Big Ten scoring leader. He had 129 points in 12 conference games to McCracken's 123.

THE 1928-29 SEASON

The senior manager preseason report described McCracken's prospects this way:

"Branch McCracken, husky offensive threat, is expected to handle the center position with ease this year. Although slightly larger than the average hardwood player, McCracken finds little difficulty in puzzling the defensive tactics of the offense and has shown considerable ability at scoring points on follow-up shots."

McCracken lived up to his billing. He finished second in the Big Ten scoring race with 100 points.

But that wasn't enough to prevent Indiana from dropping to 7-10 and 4-8.

Branch McCracken

Besides McCracken, forward Jim Strickland scored 120 points, had a game-high 20 in the Hoosiers' 37-36 overtime win over Minnesota and became IU's second All-American and first since Dean in 1921.

THE 1929-30 SEASON

McCracken did his part, scoring 206 points and reaching double figures 11 times. However, in keeping with the poor shooting typical of the era, he averaged just 23.3 percent from the field, 58.6 percent from the line.

"McCracken's drive, long frame and keen eye for the loop caused him to be feared by all opposing pivot men," wrote the Daily Student. "His long suit is his ability to get the tip-off and to get through the guards for many follow-up shots."

In the season finale against Minnesota (a 34-29 overtime win), McCracken scored eight points to finish with 146 in Big Ten play. That broke the conference record of 143 set the previous year by Purdue's Stretch Murphy.

McCracken's record lasted two seasons, until Purdue's John Wooden totaled 154.

After the season, McCracken became IU's second straight All-American.

However, the Hoosiers never recovered from an 0-4 start and finished 8-9 and 7-5.

THE 1930-33 SEASONS

Indiana struggled to a 27-26 record during this three-year stretch. This was at the height of The Great Depression and the Big Ten had passed a series of cost-cutting measures. In an effort to boost revenue, teams were allowed to play one more non-conference game, giving them six. The 12 league games remained the same.

BUILDING A NEW GYM

The time had come for a new gym. The Hoosiers had outgrown the facility built in 1916. The Fieldhouse was built on east 7th Street at a cost of $350,000. A crowd of 8,000 watched IU beat Eastern champion Pennsylvania in the Dec. 13, 1928, dedication game. The next day's Daily Student headline – CRIMSON DEDICATES GIANT FIELDHOUSE WITH 34-26 TRIUMPH – dominated the front page.

The facility had a portable hardwood floor and a lighting system consisting of 47 electric lamps, ranging from 500 to 1,500 watts, suspended from the ceiling. There were seven floodlights, three directly over the floor, two aimed at each basket.

By the late 1940s, school officials realized it was time for a new arena. However, finances delayed the vision that became the current Assembly Hall to 1972. In the meantime, a new Fieldhouse was built in 1960 at a cost of $1.7 million. Designed as an indoor practice facility, it had 10,300 seats, twice as much lighting as the old Fieldhouse, no air conditioning and a surrounding floor of dirt and sawdust.

It was not the solution.

The Fieldhouse still stands on east 7th Street. It is now known as the Wildemuth Intramural Center.

In 1932, led by forward Arnold "Sally" Suddith and All-Big Ten guard Joe Zellar, IU finished 8-10. The record wasn't unexpected.

"Coach Dean hasn't had a great deal of genuine basketball talent with which to work, but has had some boys with strong character," wrote the Bloomington World.

FALLING PRICES Hoping to boost attendance for the 1932-33 season (in the middle of The Great Depression), IU officials cut ticket prices from $1 to 40 cents. A 10-game season-ticket book cost $4.

The policy quickly paid off. In the previous season's home opener against Miami, ticket sales were just $67.50. In the opener against Wabash, ticket sales were $108.20.

In the season finale against Ohio State, the Hoosiers drew 5,000, their biggest crowd in three years.

FOREIGN AFFAIR The highlight of the 1932-33 home season was a February game against Falcon Athletic Club of Mexico City. It was part of the Mexican squad's six-week, 32-game tour. IU won 56-27 behind guard Keith Campbell's 15 points. Campbell credited his play to his "New, specially constructed, protected eye-glasses."

Meanwhile, guard Jack Heavenridge didn't play. Dean, who annually contended with second semester academic ineligibility, denied reports Heavenridge hadn't enrolled for the second semester because of "financial difficulties."

"Heavenridge is not scholastically ineligible," said Dean. "Due to the fact he was temporarily held up in registration, he was unable to play tonight, but he will be ready for Northwestern."

BIG GUYS In December of 1932, IU faced a height disadvantage against a Marquette team Dean called the "biggest in the Middle West." Marquette's starters went from 5-10 and 198 pounds to 6-6 and 205. The Hoosiers' tallest player was 6-2 William Coulter. Nobody on the roster weighed more than 192 pounds.

While Indiana lost 21-20, it finished 10-8, its most victories in five years.

BASKETBALL CRITIQUE

Looking to improve the game and deflect criticism that basketball was too strenuous, Dean conducted a season-long survey. His findings included an average of 108 interruptions a game; the average playing period without interruption was 16.3 seconds; and each game had 22 fouls, 19 jump balls, 31 center jumps and 14 free throws.

Dean concluded that basketball provided "More than ample time for the players to rest. Indeed, the game almost goes to the other extreme in the manner of interruptions and the part played by officials in games."

He and other coaches began pushing for rules changes to speed the game.

Glen Hodson

TOP SCORER Forward Glen Hodson led the Hoosiers with 133 points. He scored in double figures his last six games, with a high of 17 in a 40-28 season-ending victory over Ohio State that caused the Buckeyes to share the Big Ten title with Northwestern.

LOOKING GOOD The 1933 freshman class was described by The Daily Student as "one of the strongest freshmen squads ever assembled at Indiana University."

Future All-American Vern Huffman had led New Castle to the 1932 Indiana state high school championship. The Daily Student called him, "probably one of the greatest basketball stars Indiana high schools have ever produced." He was the driving force behind the Hoosiers' 1936 Big Ten title, Dean's third and first in eight years.

THE 1933-35 SEASONS

During this two-year stretch, IU returned to Big Ten elite status. The Hoosiers compiled a 27-13 record and finished second in 1935.

After a 13-7 showing in 1934, Indiana came back for a 14-6 mark despite the loss of Huffman, who broke his leg during football and missed the entire season. His injury left a big hole at center.

That hole was filled by 6-9 sophomore Fred "Reach" Fechtman, the tallest player in IU history at that time. Bloomington sports editor John Sembower called him a "giant sophomore center." The Washington Post described him as the "elongated lad." Despite never having played organized ball until college, Fechtman was an instant success. He finished with 120 points.

Fechtman was one of four players to score more than 100 points in the 1934-35 season, an Indiana first. The others were Kenny Gunning (166), Willard Kehrt (139) and Lester Stout (124).

The Hoosiers' 35-point average was a school record. In 11 years under Dean to that point, they'd averaged 31.5 points.

Ken Gunning led the Hoosiers in scoring in 1935 with 166 points. Gunning was named All-American in 1937.

BIG WIN Indiana certified itself as a Big Ten contender by upsetting previously unbeaten Iowa 40-35 before 9,000 fans at Iowa City. That gave the Hoosiers a share of first place with the Hawkeyes. Both teams were 3-1.

GOING TO OT Playing before 8,700 people in Madison, Wis., IU scored the final nine points of regulation to tie the score at 27 and send its game with the Badgers into overtime. However, conference scoring leader Gil McDonald scored four quick points in the extra session and Wisconsin posted a 37-27 win.

GOOD REPLACEMENT Midway through the season, guard Wendel Walker replaced co-captain Bob Porter in the starting lineup. Walker went on to make All-Big Ten. Forward Willard Kerht also made it.

BEATING PURDUE IU beat PU 41-35 before 7,000 at the Fieldhouse. Gunning, Kerht and Fechtman scored 12 points each. The victory pulled the Hoosiers into three-way tie for second at 7-3, one game behind Wisconsin.

However, IU's title hopes ended a week later with a 40-22 loss at under-achieving Northwestern.

"We were the victims of Northwestern's long-expected basketball revolution," said Dean. "We faced them when they were playing their best. In my opinion, no team in the conference could have beaten them."

Indiana finished second at 8-4.

THE 1935-36 SEASON

Huffman was back. The 6-2, 190-pound junior was coming off an outstanding football season in which he was named the Big Ten's most valuable player. He would go on to play for the NFL's Detroit Lions.

Because of the emergence of Fechtman (who had shrunk to 6-7 on the IU roster), Huffman moved to guard.

Besides Huffman, the Hoosiers returned eight lettermen. They lived up to expectations, setting a school record for victories by going 18-2 and sharing the conference title with Purdue. Both teams had 11-1 records.

Ken Gunning was the leading scorer with 183 points. Fechtman was next with 124. Huffman added 95 points.

IU opened 5-0 before DePaul pulled off a 35-31 victory. DePaul shot 48 percent from the field to Indiana's 33 percent.

The Hoosiers followed with a nine-game winning streak before Ohio State beat them 43-34. In that contest, Indiana was just 11-of-54 from the field. Fechtman led IU with 11 points. Ohio State's Warren Whitlinger had 16.

The Hoosiers closed with four straight victories, including a 40-34 win over Ohio State in the season finale. The conference crown was their first since 1928.

"We waited three years for it and we finally came through," said senior guard Wendell Walker. "The only thing I regret is that I have to leave those boys. They are a fine bunch."

HIGHLIGHTS Huffman scored 10 as IU beat Michigan 33-27 before 7,500 at Yost Field House. It was the Wolverines' first loss of year ... Gunning totaled 19 points – the most by any Hoosier that season – in a 33-30 win over Chicago. The Hoosiers played without

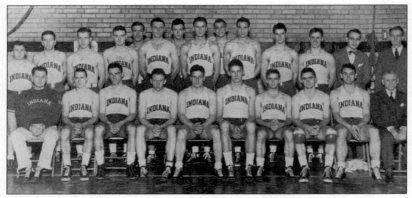

The 1936 IU team, Big Ten Co-Champions. First row, left to right: Coach Everett Dean, Robert K. Etnire, Willis E. Hosler, Charles F. Scott, co-captain Lewis W. Walker, Fred D. Fechtman, co-captain Lester L. Stout, Kenneth W. Gunning, Vernon R. Huffman, Athletic Director Zora G. Clevenger. Second row: Mr. Campbell, William Silberstein, Mr. Hobson, Joe M. Platt, Roger G. Ratliff, Mr. McNaughton, Mr. Liehr, Mr. Brooks, Mr. Anderson, Manager Bishop, Trainer Ferguson. Third row: Mr. Dittrich, Mr. Mendel, James Birr.

Fechtman, who was out with a sprained ankle … Indiana edged Wisconsin 26-24 even though Huffman and Fechtman had fouled out. Trailing 23-22 with two minutes left, the Hoosiers regained the lead on a pair of free throws by Huffman's replacement, Joe Platt. IU never trailed again.

WHO'S THE BEST Indiana and Purdue shared the title although, because of the round-robin rotation, the teams never played. Who would have won? Here's what Indianapolis Star Sports Editor W. Blaine Patton thought: "Toss a coin. The hot team would win. We have seen both combinations play several games this season and this is the best we can come up with."

MAJOR RULES CHANGES 1) Three-second rule for any offensive player staying in the lane, 2) The defensive team will get the ball under the basket after a successful free throw (instead of a jump ball), 3) More leniency on the double dribble call (under old rules, officials called a double dribble if a defensive player deflected a pass, recovered the ball and started to dribble).

What did Dean think?

"The 3-second rule in the lane is a wise rule," he said. "The free throw rule is a penalty on tall men.

"The new dribble rule will help the game in that it will make for more fast plays and will minimize or lessen officiating on that particular play. For many years, technicalities in the application of the dribble rule have robbed the game of many sensational plays and forced more whistle blowing and more officiating."

NEW UNIFORMS The Hoosiers purchased red silk uniforms. However, they only wore them on the road because Big Ten rules stipulated home teams wear white.

BASKET LIGHTS Indiana installed red lights atop each basket at the Fieldhouse. The light flashed whenever a basket was made. The purpose was to help fans sitting in bleachers directly behind the basket know when a team scored. The backboard – see-through material was decades away – blocked their view.

The Hoosiers also installed a loud-speaker system that enabled an announcer to identify players, give statistics and provide occasional play-by-play.

OLYMPIAN Dean was named to the Olympic committee to select the American basketball team. Officials decided to divide the country into regionals consisting of the top college teams. After the 1935-36 season, those teams would play for regional titles, with the winners advancing to a national tournament along with top AAU and other amateur squads. The winning team would provide some – but not all – of the players for the Olympic squad.

After the season, IU was invited to play in the Midwest Olympic regional. The other teams were DePaul, Notre Dame, Northwestern, Ohio State and Illinois. However, a week before the regional was to start, Indiana withdrew. After a meeting with school president William Lowe Bryan, the faculty committee and athletic officials, Dean announced the Hoosiers wouldn't participate because of the "loss of time to academic work." Notre Dame, Illinois, Ohio State and Northwestern also withdrew.

The Americans went on to win the gold medal in Berlin, the first time basketball was part of Olympic competition.

THE 1936-37 SEASON

The Hoosiers had eight returning lettermen, including the versatile Huffman. Dean called him "the perfect player."

Also back was Gunning, the previous season's leading scorer. Described by The Daily Student as "The Hoosiers fastest player," Gunning would make All-American. Huffman would not.

It promised to be one of Dean's best seasons. Instead, it was one of his most disappointing.

FAST START Indiana opened 8-0 with a high-powered offense that averaged 49 points. That included a 60-33 victory over Kansas State that set a Fieldhouse scoring record, breaking the 54-point total IU had achieved the previous year against Wisconsin. The Hoosiers and Kansas State combined for 145 shots, making 44.

Two weeks later, IU won at Butler 61-27 behind Gunning's 15 points.

PRIME TIME The national media took notice when the Hoosiers headed East and beat strong squads from Manhattan (42-34) and Villanova (43-28). Life Magazine did a photo shoot of the Manhattan game. News reel companies shot both games and showed them at movie houses throughout the country.

Fans began talking of an unbeaten season, although Dean expressed concern. He said the Big Ten champion would go 8-4.

In the conference opener, Iowa tried a stall and lost 28-24. Chicago tried to run with the Hoosiers and fell, 46-26.

Then reality set in. Illinois beat the Hoosiers 40-31 behind Lou Boudreau's 11 points. Boudreau later became a Hall of Fame short-stop for the Cleveland Indians.

FLOODING WATERS Purdue was next and the Jan. 16 game was in danger of being called off because of state-wide flooding. The Ohio River had over-flowed its banks, submerging Louisville and Evansville, and forcing the evacuation of Jeffersonville.

Still, the game went on and Purdue won 41-30.

FADING HOOSIERS Losses mounted. The Bloomington World wrote that "The fire is gone. The team is plagued by poor control of the tip, bad passing and poor goal shooting. Whether they have gone stale or lost some of that necessary confidence is debatable."

Indiana also was hurt by the loss of Fechtman, who ran out of eligibility after the first semester. Huffman replaced him at center. It didn't help. IU lost five of its last seven games and finished 13-7 and 6-6.

By the end, the Hoosiers were using a stall. They took just 20 shots in beating Michigan 31-27 in the season finale.

Minnesota and Illinois shared the Big Ten crown with 10-2 records.

Gunning scored a team-high 163 points. Bill Johnson was next with 142 points. Robert Etnire added 127. Sophomore Ernie Andres scored 101. Huffman had 100.

WHAT A BARGAIN The five-day trip to New York and Philadelphia cost $425. The biggest expense – $216 for meals.

1937-38 SEASON

Before 1937, games were stopped after every basket for a center jump. To speed play and boost scoring, the center jump was eliminated. The result – Big Ten scoring increased by eight points a game. Dean said it added almost four minutes of action per game.

It didn't help the Hoosiers. Dean returned only one starter – Bill Johnson. Two sophomores started: forward Jay McCreary and center Marvin Huffman (brother of Vernon).

IU took another hit when center Jim Birr was ruled ineligible in early February after he was late turning in a paper for his international business class. The Hoosiers finished 10-10 and 4-8. Although no one knew it at the time, it would be Dean's last season in Bloomington.

HEADING WEST For first time in school history, IU made a West Coast trip. The Hoosiers beat Southern California (42-39) and UCLA (42-33). Total cost for the 12-day trip was $715.

It wasn't all work. Former IU athlete Kermit Maynard had become a cowboy movie star. He got the Hoosiers photo opportunities with actress Olympe Bradna and actor Gene Raymond.

SUSPICIOUS MINDS The Daily Student reported after the Purdue victory that "Two of Purdue's players didn't become eligible until the day of the game. One of them took five tests Friday and Saturday."

ALL-AMERICAN Ernie Andres became IU's sixth All-American and fifth in eight years. The junior guard scored 250 points, including a school record 162 in Big Ten play. That broke Branch McCracken's mark of 146.

Despite a cold and an upset stomach, Andres set a conference single-game record by scoring 30 points in 45-35 win over Illinois in the season finale. Andres was 13-for-30 from the field and 4-for-5 from the line. He scored 19 second-half points.

Here's how The Daily Student described it:

> "Andres, playing the last part of the game with an injured leg after racking up 28 points, scored his last basket on a follow-up shot with one minute remaining and then was immediately replaced."

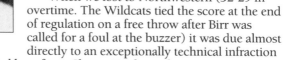

OLD COACH DOES DEAN NO FAVORS

Frustrated over a difficult season and what he felt was poor officiating, the normally calm Dean charged into the referees' locker room after IU's 38-36 loss at Purdue. The most critical statistic for him was the number of fouls – the Hoosiers were called for 11 to the Boilermakers' six.

Dean talked with reporters afterward.

"I do not make a practice of talking to basketball officials in their dressing room after a game whether we win or lose, but I'm convinced our boys didn't get a fair break from the officials in this game," he said in a Feb. 6 Daily Student story.

George Levis

"Anyone who follows basketball knows that it is impossible to play the type of pressing defense used by Purdue and get by with only six fouls.

"When we lost to Northwestern (32-29 in overtime. The Wildcats tied the score at the end of regulation on a free throw after Birr was called for a foul at the buzzer) it was due almost directly to an exceptionally technical infraction of the rules called by referee Clarno. We lost. Then we run into the brand of loose officiating that was handed out in the Purdue game.

"There must be more consistency in our officiating."

Adding to Dean's frustrations was that one of the referees was George Levis, Dean's coach his senior year at Indiana. Wrote The Bloomington Evening World; "One would think George would have given the home boys a break if anyone would get it, but no dice."

Andres bettered by one point the record set by Northwestern's Joe Rieff in 1933 and tied by Purdue's Jewell Young and Illinois' Rick Dehner. He also topped the school record of 28 set by Chester Harmeson in 1906.

"I had a bad cold, but I wouldn't have cared if I'd been sick all season if it was going to be like that," said Andres.

CARDINALS PREVAIL Ball State, under Coach Branch McCracken, upset the Hoosiers 42-38 in Muncie. It remains the Cardinals' only victory over IU in 13 meetings.

The Indianapolis Star reported that "Pupil bested teacher (when) Branch McCracken, former All-American center at Indiana, sent into action a team that was too good in the pinches for Everett Dean's Crimson squad."

It was a big moment for McCracken. But six months later, when Dean left for Stanford, McCracken had a bigger one. He was going home.

All-American Ernie Andres broke the school scoring record in 1938. Andres would later become an assistant coach.

The Branch McCracken Era

Black-and-white images grab you – the athlete Branch McCracken was; the coach he became.

In some photos, McCracken is young, powerful and ruggedly handsome; very much "The Sheriff" and "The Bear" he was affectionately called.

Branch McCracken

In others, he is weary and older than his years – hair gray, face lined and pale, eyes bespectacled; his shoulders stooped by time, failing health, fans' expectations and his own intensity.

Everett Dean brought tradition to IU. McCracken provided national renown. For more than a quarter of a century, McCracken symbolized Indiana basketball with his Hurryin' Hoosiers philosophy and a competitiveness he sometimes couldn't control.

A story goes that after one game, a fan approached McCracken and asked, "Why did they call a technical foul on Indiana?"

"Indiana had too many men on the floor," said McCracken.

"Who was the sixth man?"

"Me," said McCracken.

With the exception of Bob Knight, no IU coach had as much influence as McCracken. His fastbreak style – in contrast to Dean's deliberate approach – produced two national championships and four Big Ten titles. His success, longevity and warm personality made him an Indiana legend.

"Everett was here for 14 years and won three Big Ten championships," Knight told The Indianapolis Star in 1992. "Then Branch took it one step further and won two national championships and in doing so, created and maintained a level of interest in Indiana college basketball, and particularly at Indiana University, that is really the foundation of the interest we have today."

McCracken's teams won national titles in 1940 and

Branch McCracken conducted a practice with the same intensity he utilized while coaching a game.

'53; Big Ten crowns in 1953, '54, '57 and '58. He won national coach-of-the-year honors in '40 and '53. His 24-year record was 364-174, including 210-116 in the Big Ten. Three years of military service in the mid-1940s because of World War II prevented it from being better.

McCracken was inducted into the Naismith Memorial Basketball Hall of Fame as a player in 1960. He was in the first class inducted into the IU Athletic Hall of Fame in 1982.

"Whenever I hear the word 'Hoosier,' I think of Mac," said former Indiana All-American Bob Leonard, who played on the '53 title team. "He was what I term the real homespun Hoosier. His personality transcended the population of entire states."

BREAKING THE COLOR BARRIER In 1947, McCracken brought in the Big Ten's first black basketball player, Shelbyville High School all-star Bill Garrett.

"There's no rule against colored athletes," McCracken told the Indianapolis News in 1946. "But somebody has to be the first to use them. It's going to be me."

The next year, it was.

"It wasn't as hard a thing for me as it was for Bill," McCracken told the Lafayette Journal and Courier in 1970, shortly before his death. "All of the pressure was on him.

Branch McCracken with Bill Garrett, the first black player in the Big Ten.

"But he was an exceptional guy. He handled discrimination on and off the floor without changing expression."

THE LEGEND Archie Dees, another former Indiana All-American, once said he came to Bloomington because "(McCracken) was a legend and I thought it would be something to play for a legend. He was a great psychologist and motivator. He was a competitor and hated to lose."

MR. INTENSITY McCracken kept his edge by drinking as many as six cups of coffee a day. During a game against Duquesne in 1939, he smashed his hand through two chairs. After the Hoosiers swept the season series from Purdue in 1940, the first time that had ever happened, a pumped up McCracken couldn't relax. He walked seven miles, until 3 the next morning, before finally heading home.

"They talk about how tough Bob Knight is," Leonard once told Indianapolis Star columnist Bill Benner. "Well, Bob Knight is no tougher than Branch McCracken, I'll guarantee you that."

McCracken's practices were famous for their running. Players ran cross country in the fall, then sprinted to exhaustion once the season began.

"Branch kept the weight off you," said former player and eventual successor Lou Watson. "He'd run you to death."

RIVAL COACHES McCracken sometimes got on the nerves of Purdue's Piggy Lambert, also a feisty coach. Lambert once told McCracken to be more calm, saying he was "too young."

McCracken's response – Lambert was "too old."

INNOVATOR McCracken was one of the first coaches to use air travel (the Hoosiers flew to their West Coast trip in 1940) and in permitting live television of his entire home schedule (starting in 1949 on Bloomington's WTTV).

In the early 1960s, concern about high-scoring games and dominating big men caused some coaches to suggest raising the basket to 12 feet. McCracken had another idea.

"Don't raise the basket, that makes it tough on the little 6-3 fellow. Instead, make the hoop smaller."

YOU CAN'T PLEASE EVERYONE McCracken's success provided no protection from critics who first labeled him too young, then too old. His fast-break style made him a target. In his 1955 book, "Indiana Basketball," McCracken defended it.

"I have always used this style of ball because I have felt this was what the average boy likes to play. Naturally, we are going to make more mistakes playing this style than we would playing a slow, deliberate game. However, we feel we more than compensate for the mistakes by getting many more scoring opportunities."

IN THE BEGINNING McCracken developed his uptempo preference as a standout at Monrovia, Ind. He learned to play, so the story goes, by

McCracken's love for coffee helped to keep him on the edge of the bench during games. He put a high priority on education during practice and in the classroom.

tossing a stuffed pig bladder at a barnyard barrel hoop.

By the time he arrived at IU (another legend had it that he came without shoes because "that's the way he played"), the 6-4, 215-pound McCracken had developed into an imposing player. He once held the Big Ten single-season scoring record, with 146 points in 1930. He averaged 12.2 points that season and was named All-American.

McCracken's talents included football. He was a three-year starting end for the Hoosiers and was offered a contract by the Green Bay Packers. He turned it down

Although he had once had ideas about becoming a veterinarian (another of his nicknames was "Doc"), studies didn't always top his priority list and teammates sometimes had to rouse him to make class. That experience caused him to make sure his own players attended class. His players' graduation rate was one of the nation's highest.

MUNCIE BOUND After graduating in 1930, McCracken played pro basketball briefly. In 1931, he became the head coach at Ball State, compiling a seven-year record of 93-41. That included a 42-38 victory over Indiana in December of 1937, still the Cardinals' only win over the Hoosiers. During his stay in Muncie, he married Mary Jo Pittinger, the daughter of the Ball State president.

In the summer of 1938, when Dean left for Stanford, McCracken was his unanimous successor.

IMPRESSIVE DEBUT

In that first season of 1938-39, the Hoosiers were 17-3, IU's second-most victories in a season. McCracken was named Big Ten coach of the year.

Indiana started strong, winning its first seven games before losing at Ohio State, 45-38. The Hoosiers then won 10 more in a row and were poised to win the conference title. But season-ending road losses to Purdue (45-34) and Michigan (53-43) dropped IU to second, a game behind Ohio State.

RAE OF LIGHT The Michigan loss provided a story McCracken enjoyed retelling:

"The Wolverines had a big center named Rae who was so hot, he couldn't miss. All through the first half and well into the second I sat on the bench and watched our best defensive man's futile attempts to check Rae. I sent in fresh players. No success. Rae continued to run wild.

"Finally, with tears in my eyes, and knowing the game to be already lost, I turned to a rangy, raw sophomore who hadn't seen action all season. 'Tom,' I said, 'do me a favor. Get out there and keep Rae from scoring any more baskets these last two minutes.'

A cocky look on his face, the boy started for the scorer's table. Just as he got there, he turned and yelled, 'Hey, Coach, which one is Rae?' "

NO TIME TO BE MEEK McCracken wanted aggressive play. Following a loss, he often checked the foul totals ahead of points or rebounds. He believed a player who scored a lot of points, but committed few fouls, wasn't trying his best.

That attitude didn't endear McCracken to opposing coaches. A rival once accused him of encouraging rough play.

"No I don't," he replied, "But I don't discourage it."

THE FIRST NCAA CHAMPIONSHIP

Marvin Huffman was captain of the 1940 NCAA Championship team.

McCracken's fast-break style became a permanent fixture following a loss to Minnesota during the 1939-40 season. Trailing 29-13 at halftime, author Jack Miller, in American Boy Magazine, relayed the following locker room conversation.

"We've tried deliberate basketball against these fellows and it doesn't work," said McCracken. "This second half, let's drive. Let's run 'em right out of the Fieldhouse."

Captain Marvin Huffman agreed.

"Come on, gang, let's go. Minnesota thinks they've got a firewagon outfit. We'll show them what speed really is."

In eight minutes, IU went on 20-1 run to take a 33-30 lead. That Minnesota's Willie Warhol hit a halfcourt shot at the buzzer for a 46-44 victory didn't change McCracken's mind about the merits of the fastbreak.

"After that," wrote Miller, "Indiana gave up slow-breaking attacks. They became speed merchants and speed merchants they are today."

With 12 returning lettermen, McCracken had experience with that speed. There were Bill and Bob Menke at center; Marvin Huffman and Bob Dro at guards; Curley Armstrong, Herman Schaefer and Jay McCreary (back after sitting out a year) at forward.

There was even sophomore Andy Zimmer, who was once told by PU's Piggy Lambert he was "too skinny and frail" for Big Ten basketball. The 6-4, 180-pounder shrugged off a preseason practice collision that knocked out two teeth to take over the center position. That allowed Bill Menke to move to forward and strengthened the Hoosiers' already impressive depth.

POTENT OFFENSE IU scored 519 points in 12 Big Ten games to break by seven Purdue's conference record set the year before.

BATTLE OF UNBEATENS Indiana was 9-0 and Illinois was 7-0 when the teams met in the Big Ten opener. The Illini were without All-Big Ten guard Bill Hapac, who was sick. IU won 38-36 when Illinois forward Colin Handlon missed a layup at the buzzer.

HIGHLIGHTS In an NCAA Tournament preview, Bill Menke scored 22 in IU's 51-49 victory over Duquesne ... During a 10-day period in late December, without a practice, Indiana beat Butler, Duquesne and Villanova ... The Hoosiers rallied from a 10-point halftime deficit to beat Iowa 46-42 ... In a 57-30 victory over Michigan, McCracken became the first conference coach to use every player (21) in a game ... Northwestern edged Indiana 40-36 to drop the Hoosiers out of a first-place tie with Purdue. There were 44 fouls called ... A 44-26 loss to Ohio State in March cost the Hoosiers a

The 1940 Indiana team won the school's first NCAA Championship in only the second year of the NCAA Basketball Tournament.

share at the conference championship. Without McCreary, who was bedridden with a high fever, Indiana shot just 16 percent from the field ... IU ended the season with a 52-31 victory over Ohio State to extend its home-court winning streak to 19.

BOILERS SWEPT For the first time since the series started in 1901, Indiana swept a season series from Purdue, 46-39 in Bloomington and 51-45 in West Lafayette. They were Purdue's only Big Ten losses.

CAGED COURTS To protect players from falling into bleachers, courts were ringed by safety nets. The Indianapolis News wrote that IU was on the cutting edge of that technology.

"Indiana's court has been dressed up for the year. Eight additional high-powered lights have been hung over the playing floor and hard-rubber posts have been installed to hold the boundary net instead of the wooden stakes which were threats to players forced out of bounds. They are the first rubber posts of their kind."

ON THE ATTACK McCracken preached "free-lance" to his players.

"All we care about is getting the ball in the enemy basket in the shortest possible time. Our emphasis is on rolling up those points. Our defense lies primarily in our offense. `Go! Go! Go!' is our watch-word."

FORGET THE SET SHOT McCracken had his players shoot hundreds of

STREAMLINING THE BACKBOARD

In an effort to help the game and fans, McCracken proposed a new type of backboard in the Jan. 18, 1940 edition of The Indianapolis News:

"Branch McCracken, Indiana's basketball coach, thinks the present type backboard is out of date. In its place, the Indiana mentor proposes a "streamlined" board of smaller size and altered shape. The board would be cut from four feet to 3 and 1/2 feet high, and from six to five feet in width....

"The new board would eliminate the corners and replace them with beveled edges. Saying the corners are not used by shooters, Mac sees a board of slightly oval shape with straight edges between the rounded corners. The hoop would set at the bottom edge instead of six inches above as it does now.

" 'There is no need for a backboard of the present size,' said McCracken. 'The corners are not used and the six-inch strip below the basket hoop is worthless.'

"The smaller board, McCracken believes, would increase the range of vision for spectators sitting in the end seats and lessen the danger of tall players hitting the bottom of it and would place more emphasis on skillful shooting."

what were then known as "one-handed shots."

"No defense has ever been devised to halt this type of shooting," he said.

THE NCAA TOURNAMENT Indiana finished a game behind Purdue in the Big Ten race. However, the Hoosiers had a better overall record (17-3 to 16-4) and had beaten the Boilermakers twice. That was enough for the selection committee (there were no automatic bids), which picked IU to represent the Midwest.

"Butler's Tony Hinkle was on the NCAA committee then and later told me we were picked over Purdue because we had the best team," Dro told Inside Indiana years later.

The NCAA Tournament was in its infancy and not all teams were excited about playing – or paying. The tourney cost McCracken income from 15 speaking engagements and prevented him from attending the Indiana state high school finals for the first time in 19 years. IU lost $133 on the finals in Kansas City.

According to an Indianapolis News story on March 7, "Coach McCracken was hot about the idea (playing in the NCAA tourney) at first, but had cooled off some. It is believed Indiana might be forced to accept. Ohio State was last year. It was learned here today that Purdue was eager to avoid being chosen, but the committee voted for Indiana considering IU's record better. The faculty may agree, with the stipulation that the tournament be played in the Butler Fieldhouse rather than New York."

The site was switched from New York to Butler. The teams were IU (17-3), Springfield College (16-2), Duquesne (19-2) and Western Kentucky (24-5). Ticket prices ranged from 65 cents to $1.10.

Bob Dro

NO TROUBLE With Herman Schaefer scoring a game-high 14 points, IU cruised over Springfield in the opening game, 48-24.

Only Duquense stood between Indiana and the finals. Duquense's losses had come against Indiana and then Colorado in the recently concluded NIT title game (teams could play in both tournaments then). Bill Menke scored 10 points as the Hoosiers won 39-30 to advance to Kansas City.

THE SHOWDOWN United Press described Kansas as a "horse and buggy team," while IU had a "firewagon style."

Said McCracken: "Kansas will just have to produce a lot of basketball to beat us. I think it will be close."

Here's how the Indianapolis Star reported IU's 60-42 victory:

"Jay McCreary, a gum-chewing blond midget in a forest of physical giants, poured in 12 points as Indiana University defeated the University of Kansas for the basketball title...

"McCreary did not start for the Hoosiers, but once he got onto the floor, he made Coach Branch McCracken realize the oversight."

Huffman, who also scored 12 points, won the Final Four Outstanding Player Award. It was, said Dro, a deserving achievement for IU's toughest player.

"I'm telling you," said Dro years later in an Akron Beacon Journal story, "if you were slacking off, not playing your best, you had better watch him – because he'd punch you. You did your best or you had to face him."

Huffman received a gold medal for his Final Four award. All the Hoosiers got gold watches, gold basketballs and a pair of shoes.

Southern California coach Sam Barry, whose team was ranked No. 1 for most of the season before being upset by Kansas in the NCAA semifinals, was impressed with IU's performance.

"I knew Indiana was fast, but not that fast," said Barry. "McCracken will be a guy not to schedule until some of those boys graduate."

THE 1940-41 SEASON

With every key player back but Huffman, IU was favored to win the Big Ten title and its second straight national championship.

To prepare the Hoosiers, McCracken put together a rigorous pre-conference schedule that included a four-game West Coast trip.

Jay McCreary helped lead the Hoosiers to the 1940 NCAA Championship.

A key early matchup came against Stanford and Coach Everett Dean. Bill Menke hit a 17-foot shot in overtime to give the Hoosiers a 60-59 victory.

STREAK ENDS On Dec. 27, the Hoosiers lost to Southern California, 41-39. The Trojans scored three points in the last minute to break a 38-38 tie and snap IU's 26-game winning streak against non-conference opponents. That dated to Dec. 21, 1937, during Dean's final season as coach, when Bradley Tech beat the Hoosiers 50-39.

IU rebounded to beat UCLA 51-26 the next day, then traveled to New Orleans for a matchup with Kentucky in the Sugar Bowl Classic. The Hoosiers won 48-45, prompting UK Coach Adolph Rupp to call McCracken "one of the greatest young coaches in the nation."

BIG TEN ROLL Bill Menke scored 24 points as the Hoosiers opened Big Ten play with a 48-38 win over Illinois. They won their first three

Brothers Bill Menke (left) and Bob Menke (right) with teammate Norm Halser. All hailed from Huntingburg, Ind.

games before Purdue upset them in West Lafayette, 40-36.

Indiana rebounded to win five straight. That included its first victory at Ohio State in 10 years.

Menke was the main force with a shooting style that the Fort Wayne Journal-Gazette described as "one-handed shots, most of them from a flat-footed position resembling the stance of a shot putter."

Menke wound up with a team-high 176 points. His three-year total of 532 points broke the school record of 525 set by McCracken.

He got plenty of help from Dro, who made Look Magazine's All-American team.

UNBEATEN NO MORE On Feb. 24, 1941, Wisconsin defeated IU in Bloomington, 38-30, to win the conference championship. It was the first home loss for McCracken, snapping a 27-game streak. IU shot just 12-for-78 from the field.

The victory gave the Badgers the NCAA Tournament bid. They went on to win the national title.

IU, the Big Ten runner-up for the third straight season with a 17-3 overall record (10-2 in the league), went nowhere.

"There's no question about my biggest heartbreak," McCracken told the Indianapolis Star after his retirement. "That was when Bud Foster, the Wisconsin coach and one of my best friends, beat us in Bloomington to win the league. They went on to win the NCAA and that kept us from possibly getting two NCAA titles in a row."

THE 1941-42 SEASON

Andy Zimmer was the only returning starter. The Hoosiers were boosted by the arrival of sharp-shooting swingman Ralph Hamilton, one of 14 sophomores on the squad.

"Perhaps only in height will our team this season compare in any way with the squad which performed so well for us for three years," McCracken told the Indianapolis Times on Dec. 2, 1941. "...We'll be young and inexperienced and lucky to finish in the first division."

IU was more than lucky, going 15-6 overall and 10-5 in the Big Ten to finish second for the fourth straight year. Along the way, they beat defending national champion Wisconsin and eventual Big Ten champ Illinois.

In order to boost income, the number of conference games was increased from 12 to 15.

WORLD-CLASS WORRIER (according to a Daily Student story on Dec. 17, 1941) – "On nights before big games, (McCracken) is said to complete the equivalent of two or three 14-mile hikes – all within his own home. Sleep is out of the question. It is much more soothing to walk, and worry....Not until early dawn do his pacings cease."

The Indianapolis Star later recounted an episode following IU's 40-39 win over Purdue. The game was rebroadcast on an Indianapolis radio station and McCracken was anxious to hear it.

"McCracken could hardly wait until the rebroadcast started," wrote The Star. "He paced the living room floor, fidgeted with dials and really gave the parlor rug a beating with his nervous, jumpy strides.

"It didn't matter to McCracken that the game had already been won. He cocked his ear at the radio loudspeaker and followed every shot and dribble. Amid squirms and jerky explosive moments, he listened right down to the last shot and then went into a semi-collapse at the finish."

TOUGH GAME McCracken's anxiety wasn't helped by the Purdue game's roughness. The Bloomington Telephone described it this way:

"It was the wildest, roughest, most sensational battle in all of the 67 games between the two Hoosier rivals. Some fouls were called, but most got by officials Rollie Branum of Wisconsin and Earl Townsend of Michigan.

"On one occasion, Indiana's Johnny

Johnny Logan, a tough Hoosier who backed down from no one.

Logan was taking on half the Purdue bench when some of the Boilermaker subs tried to hold the ball which had gone out of bounds. On another occasion, Andy Zimmer and (Purdue's) Mickey 'hot head' Tierney reached the fist-to-head stage and had to be separated.

"When the explosion of the timer's gun brought stark reality to Purdue and ecstasy to Indiana, two very unpopular officials tried to make for cover. But Earl Townsend was a trifle slow and he was swarmed in by a host of Black and Gold players. According to observers, Purdue guard Don Blanken swung a hard right off Mr. Townsend's handsome chin."

THE 1942-43 SEASON

America's entry into World War II began draining the college game of players and coaches.

On Feb. 24, reserve Bob Cowan was ordered to report to the Army Air Corps. Most of the other players, and McCracken, were called into service by the fall of 1943.

The war had other affects. Gasoline and tire rationing hurt crowds. After a victory at Iowa, the Hoosiers' bus trip home was delayed outside of Bloomington for nearly half an hour because of a

AN INTERVIEW WITH MCCRACKEN

Even a coach as media friendly as McCracken sometimes had trouble with reporters. Here is a Feb. 4 interview between a Bloomington World reporter and McCracken for a preview of the game with Illinois. The Illini were leading the Big Ten with a 7-0 record. At 5-3, IU was fighting to get back into contention.

Reporter: "You sound awfully good, coach."

McCracken: "I'm feeling good, yeah, yeah."

Reporter: "Cooking anything special for Illinois?"

McCracken: "Little defense maybe."

Reporter: "Nothing special though, huh?"

McCracken: "Nope, nope. Nothing special, I guess."

Reporter: "The boys looked good at Ohio State, huh (46-43 IU win)?"

McCracken: "Yeah, yeah."

Reporter: "The game with Illinois should be a pretty high scoring affair, don't you think, coach?"

McCracken: "Well, could be."

Reporter: "Are the boys shooting for this one?"

McCracken: "That's a silly question to ask, isn't it?"

Reporter: "Yeah, yeah."

McCracken: "Think we can beat 'em?"

Reporter: "Oh sure coach."

McCracken: "I'll see ya."

Indiana did win, 41-36, although it didn't stop the Illini from winning the conference title.

Monroe County blackout.

The war didn't hurt IU's performance. The Hoosiers won their first 16 games and built a school-record 17-game winning streak over two seasons.

With Indiana and Illinois both undefeated, and because the teams weren't schedule to play, Indianapolis Star Sports Editor W. Blaine Patton wrote an open letter to Major John L. Griffith, commissioner of the Big Ten, asking him to schedule a postseason game between the teams.

Griffith declined.

Wisconsin ended the Hoosiers' streak with a 57-53 victory. Indiana lost at Purdue 41-38 in the season finale to finish 18-2 and 11-2. Illinois won the Big Ten crown with a 12-0 mark.

RECORD GAME Hamilton scored 31 points – breaking Ernie Andres' school record by one – as Indiana beat Iowa 71-55 on Jan. 23. Hamilton had 13 field goals and five free throws. His 249 season points just missed Andres' school mark of 250 set in 1938.

"Hamilton came to us with a great basket eye, and he's improved that," said McCracken. "He's a fine rebounder, a good team player."

Also in that game, IU broke the Big Ten's single-game scoring record. The Hoosiers' 71 points were two more than the mark held by Illinois and Purdue.

TOUGH FINISH Tempers flared in the season-ending loss to Purdue. According to the Daily Student, IU's Johnny Logan and Purdue's Max Biggs got into a scuffle after Biggs tackled Logan on a fast break. In the ensuing brawl, the Hoosiers' Ward Williams suffered a black eye. Williams recovered and finished with a game-high 11 points.

MAY NOT BE BACK McCracken, the day before the season finale against Purdue and three days before he would join the Navy, told the Indianapolis News he might not return to coaching.

No one believed him.

HARRY C. GOOD

In the spring of 1943, Navy Lt. Branch McCracken took a leave of absence to serve in World War II. In August, school officials announced his

Coach turned soldier, Branch McCracken served his country during World War II.

The Indiana squad of 1944-45 with substitute Coach Harry C. Good.

replacement: Harry C. Good, who had a 15-year record of 192-52 record at Indiana Central College (now the University of Indianapolis).

IU officials convinced Good to take over until McCracken returned. Good also favored a fast-break style. From December of 1940 to January of 1942, his Indiana Central teams won 30 consecutive games. In 1942, Indiana Central was ranked ninth in the nation, the only small school listed in the top 10.

FIRST SEASON With graduation and World War II taking all the players from the previous season, Good knew the Hoosiers would struggle.

"We know we'll be out-classed in almost every game," said Good. "The boys have a lot to learn."

With a roster of one senior and 10 freshmen, the Hoosiers finished with 7-15. Paul Shields scored a team-high 178 points.

THE 1944-45 SEASON The talent was better, although Good had no idea how long it would last. All his players were subject to the draft at any time. After 14 games, leading scorer Gene Faris was inducted into the Army. Center Al Kralovansky took advantage to finish with a team-high 195 points, six more than Faris.

Indiana finished 10-11.

TURNING DOWN THE NCAA The Hoosiers went 18-3 in the 1945-46 season. Their 9-3 conference mark put them second behind Ohio State (10-2). Because of a better overall record, IU received the NCAA Tournament bid. However, the Hoosiers turned it down because center

Johnny Wallace scored a school-record 302 points in the 1944-45 season.

Tom Schwartz had been inducted into the Army and wouldn't be able to play.

Ohio State (16-5) went instead.

POTENT SCORER Ex-Navy bomber navigator Johnny Wallace, who two years earlier had crash landed in the English Channel during a mission, was the Hoosiers' leading scorer. He totaled a school-record 302 points and averaged almost 15 points a game. He had a season-high 27 against Butler.

LAST HURRAH Everyone knew McCracken would be back, so the players dedicated the season finale against Iowa to Good.

"We're going to win this one for you, coach," promised Kralovansky.

IU fulfilled that promise with a 49-46 victory that snapped Iowa's 18-game home-court winning streak. Good left IU with a 35-29 record. He went on to coach at Nebraska.

BIG CROWDS Big Ten teams set attendance records. The average of 7,748 for league games broke the mark of 5,800 set the previous season. Indiana averaged 2,574 in its 10 home games.

MAC IS BACK

McCracken returned after a three-year absence. His hair had turned almost completely gray, although the gray had not yet touched his dark eyebrows.

Also back after three years of military service were Hamilton, Williams and Don Ritter.

During that time, Hamilton had continued playing basketball. The previous year, he had scored almost 1,000 points for Atlanta Army Service Depot, including a game-high of 60.

Williams had played very little, and that had been two years ago.

Branch McCracken

The Hoosiers also had the services of freshman Lou Watson, who had spent the previous three years in the service (and was part of the Allied invasion of Normandy). Almost 23, he was able to play because of the wartime freshmen waiver.

It was a difficult year. Indiana struggled early, losing four straight games and five of six at one point. However, the Hoosiers rebounded to finish 12-8 and 8-4. It was yet another conference runnerup for McCracken.

Hamilton won All-American honors at guard. He set the school record for most career points (646, topping Bill Menke's total of 549). He also led the Big Ten in shooting percentage, at 37.7.

BIG CROWDS A record 7,631 saw IU win its home opener, 69-46 over Wabash. A week later, 9,330 packed the Fieldhouse as Notre Dame beat the Hoosiers 70-60.

NEW TRADITION Officials announced the IU-PU winner would receive the Fire Bell Trophy. A blue key would be attached to the trophy for IU victories, an iron key for Purdue wins.

THE 1947-48 SEASON

McCracken got his first taste of losing. Despite being a preseason Big Ten favorite, the Hoosiers slumped to 8-12 and 3-9. They finished last in the conference for the first time since 1915.

Don "Tex" Ritter, nicknamed for the cowboy movie star, led Indiana with 275 points, a 13.7 average.

IU lost six games by five points or less. One of the most difficult was a 51-49 loss to Purdue at the Fieldhouse. The Hoosiers led until the final minute, when the Boilermakers pulled it out.

"(Purdue's) Howie Williams was knocked on the floor and he was sitting on the floor when the ball came to him and he threw up the shot that beat us," Watson told the Bloomington Herald-Times years later. "Sittin' on the floor!"

It was that kind of year.

"I thought we had what it takes in this league and look what happened," said Mac.

THE 1948-49 SEASON

The Hoosiers set conference records for most fouls, which prevented them from doing better than 14-8 and 6-6.

The leading scorer was 6-2 sophomore center Bill Garrett, who averaged 11 points. He scored in double figures 12 times.

Garrett, the Big Ten's first black player, was popular with his teammates. They joked that he was so relaxed he would fall asleep while his ankles were being taped. They called him "Bones" because of his slender frame. However, prejudice was no joke. The players refused to eat at restaurants that wouldn't serve Garrett and protected him when situations turned nasty.

Garrett's performance wasn't a surprise. As a high school senior at Shelbyville, he had won Mr. Basketball honors and led his team to the state championship.

Garrett was one of three sophomores –Bill

Sophomore Bill Garrett led the Hoosiers in scoring in the 1948-49 season.

MCCRACKEN LOSES LOVELLETTE

(according to a 1954 Collier's story)

By late summer of 1948, McCracken thought he had locked up 6-9 Clyde Lovellette of Terre Haute. Lovellette was staying in Bloomington and was set to start classes as a freshman. But then, just before he was supposed to enroll, Lovellette asked if he could return to Terre Haute to pick up some clothes.

"Go ahead son," said McCracken, "but hurry right back."

That was the last McCracken heard of Lovellette until a wire-service story 10 days later reported Lovellette had enrolled at Kansas. Lovellette became an All-American and led Kansas to the 1952 national championship.

Clyde Lovellette

Tosheff and Gene Ring were the others – who cracked the starting lineup in McCracken's youth movement.

Veterans had their moments. In his final college game, Don Ritter scored 20 against Illinois. Lou Watson was the team's second-leading scorer with a 9.8 average.

Indiana started strong, winning its first six games and eight of its first nine. But a four-game losing streak cost the Hoosiers a shot at the Big Ten title. They came back to win four straight heading into the season finale against Illinois.

BAD ENDING Illinois routed Indiana 91-68. The combined 159 points broke the Big Ten record of 152 set by Purdue and Illinois in 1948.

The Illini's 31 free throws surpassed the conference record of 26 by Wisconsin.

THE 1949-50 SEASON

McCracken's Big Ten title expectations were boosted by a 10-0 start that saw the Hoosiers soar to No. 4 in the country.

IU's success came from its high-powered offense. The Hoosiers set a school record by averaging 64.5 points. Their 31.2 shooting percentage was described in papers as "sparkling."

McCracken's only concern was a lack of height. Nobody on the roster was taller than 6-4 and the 6-2 Garrett still played center.

Height didn't bother Garrett. He again led the team with a 12.9 scoring average. He had a high of 20 points against Arkansas. His jumper with seven seconds left gave IU a 61-59 victory over Wisconsin.

Watson, who averaged 12.2 points, had the Hoosiers' biggest offensive game with 26 against Michigan.

DOUBLEHEADER In December, IU played at Oregon State on consecutive nights, winning 65-60 and 58-53. McCracken agreed to the doubleheader to help Oregon State debut its new $1.8 million Fieldhouse.

THE BUBBLE BURSTS The Hoosiers' first loss came amid controversy. Host Michigan won 69-67 on Charley Murray's tip-in at the buzzer.

With three seconds left, IU had deflected the ball out of bounds. Big Ten rules stated that in the final two minutes, the timer couldn't stop the clock unless officials signal him to do so.

Although there was no apparent signal, the timer stopped the clock. The Wolverines inbounded the ball to Don McIntosh. His short shot was tipped in by Murray.

Hoosiers surrounded officials and the scorer to see if the basket should count. Officials ruled it did.

According to a Daily Student story on Jan. 11, 1950, "If the Wolverine time-keeper had not stopped the clock, there probably wouldn't have been time for Don McIntosh to even fire at the basket, let alone Charley Murray's winning tip-in.

"The Michigan time-keeper said that one of the officials signaled him to stop the clock when the ball went out of bounds, but both officials later denied giving the signal."

Said McCracken: "The timekeeper admitted stopping the clock when Bill Tosheff knocked the ball out of bounds with three seconds left, but the officials decided that the basket by Michigan would count and that is all there is to it."

COACHING IS TOO TOUGH Five days later, Iowa edged the visiting Hoosiers 65-64. Afterward, drained Iowa coach Pops Harrison decided to take a year's sabbatical. He said watching McCracken agonize on the sidelines quickened his decision.

WHAT MIGHT HAVE BEEN Indiana finished 17-5 overall and 7-5 in the Big Ten. Its five losses come by a total of 20 points.

Lou Watson set school and Big Ten records in scoring. He would later replace McCracken as the basketball team coach.

RECORD CAREER Watson finished his four-year career with school records in total points (757) and Big Ten points (484). He topped Ralph Hamilton's three-year totals of 646 and 426. He was a two-time all-conference choice and made All-American as a senior.

"Lou felt the pressure of the responsibility I put on him, and our season record of 17 victories in 22 games against teams consistently taller than us tells more than anything else about what a great job he did," said McCracken. "It was like having a coach on the floor to have Lou in the lineup."

THE 1950-51 SEASON

For the seventh time a Branch McCracken team finished second in the Big Ten. The Hoosier's 12-2 league record (19-3 overall) put them one game behind Illinois.

The losses all came on the road – 64-62 to Bradley, 61-54 to Minnesota and 71-65 to Illinois.

REBOUND RECORD The Hoosiers set a Big Ten mark by grabbing 89 rebounds in a 68-53 home victory over Purdue.

ALL-AMERICAN Billy Garrett wrapped up an outstanding career by making All-American. He set a new school career record of 792 points.

After leading IU in scoring and rebounding for the third straight year, Garrett went on to play for the Harlem Globetrotters before becoming a coach. He guided Indianapolis Crispus Attucks to the 1959 state championship. He died in 1974 at age 45 of a heart attack.

THE 1951-52 SEASON

Don Schlundt debuted and scoring was never the same. The 6-10 center played as a freshman because of the Korean War waiver.

Schlundt, who once scored 58 points in a high school game, was considered one of the country's top prospects. His growth spurt – in one year he went from 5-5 to 6-3 – became fodder for a series of stories, some even true. One said he grew so fast one summer he outgrew three different pair of winter pants without ever trying one of them on.

Schlundt had planned to enroll at Kentucky, but changed his mind after meeting McCracken.

"Adolph Rupp was at his height around that time and that made an impression on you," Schlundt related years later in an IU basketball game program. "But after I visited Indiana, my mind was made up. You couldn't ask for a finer coach or man than Branch McCracken."

The story went that an excited McCracken, after learning of Schlundt's decision, ran into a business professor.

Don Schlundt brought height and scoring prowess to the Indiana Hoosiers.

"I've got this great basketball prospect who is also a fine scholar," said McCracken.

"How do you know he's a fine scholar?" asked the professor.

"Well, he's 6-9, isn't he?" McCracken answered.

Using an "ambidextrous hook shot," Schlundt went on to win three straight Big Ten scoring titles. His numerous offensive records included 1,451 Big Ten points (400 more than then-runnerup Paul Ebert of Ohio State), most points in a game (47, both against Ohio State, in 1954 and '55), most career points (2,192), season average (27.1), most free throws in a game (25 against Ohio State in 1955), single season field goal percentage (50.4 in 1954), career scoring average (23.3) and most consecutive free throws in a game without a miss (14-for-14 against Minnesota on Feb. 8, 1954).

It took 32 years before Steve Alford broke Schlundt's point record. Schlundt ranks third behind Calbert Cheaney (2,613) and Alford (2,438)

Schlundt wasn't an instant success. He struggled to beat out 6-10 Lou Scott for the starting position, then scored just six points in his college debut against Valparaiso.

Still, Schlundt and Bobby Leonard helped Indiana to an 8-0 start. But the Hoosiers never recovered from a three-game road losing streak and finished 16-6 and 9-5.

Schlundt totaled a school-record 376 points, a 17.1 average. That included a school-record 35-point effort against Purdue, topping Ralph Hamilton's nine-year-old 31-point mark.

Leonard added 319 points, a 14.5 average. No one else averaged in double figures.

ANOTHER RECORD For the fifth time in two years, IU sets a new school scoring mark. The Hoosiers beat Northwestern 96-85. The 181 total points was a conference record.

Don Schlundt's hook shot was unstoppable and helped him win three straight Big Ten scoring titles.

ANOTHER CHAMPIONSHIP SEASON

McCracken had a career season. His Hoosiers won their first undisputed Big Ten championship (becoming the last conference team to do so), his first league title, and a second national crown. They had a record 17-game winning streak and finished 23-3.

It was IU's first conference title since 1936, when Everett Dean was coaching.

The Hoosiers had it all: inside power with 6-10 Don Schlundt, outside prowess with guard Bob Leonard, rebounding muscle with forward Charlie Kraak, inside defense with Dick Farley, perimeter hustle with Burke Scott, and the nation's top sixth man, Dick White.

Leonard, a two-time All-American, was IU's second-leading scorer with a 17.7 average. He would go on to play and coach professionally. He led the Indiana Pacers to three ABA titles in the 1970s and still broadcasts their games.

"For his size, Leonard was the greatest basketball player I've ever seen," White later told Inside Indiana. "He was a great outside shooter. We were a run-and-gun team that liked to fast break. I always said that if we were on a fast break, the surest way to get a bucket was to get the ball into Leonard's hands. He'd find a way to score."

If Leonard didn't, Schlundt did. He averaged 25.4 points.

Bob Leonard was an All-American at Indiana. He is now better known for his "Boom Baby" calls during Indiana Pacer games.

"Schlundt was incredible," said White. "He was a great scorer and an excellent free throw shooter. He used his 6-10 body and had a great left arm he used to perfection in holding off defenders when shooting."

RECORD ROUT The Hoosiers opened with a 95-56 blowout of Valparaiso, the most decisive season-opening win in school history. The previous best was a 46-13 win over Cincinnati in 1936.

TOUGH LOSSES Indiana lost its next two games, 71-70 at Notre Dame and 82-80 at Kansas State.

Against Notre Dame, IU lost when Irish guard Jack Stephens raced the length of the court for a layup in the last two seconds.

Notre Dame had dedicated the game to assistant coach Mickey O'Conner, hospitalized in critical condition with polio (this was the worst year of the epidemic; 58,000 Americans contracted the disease and 3,000 died). Coach Johnny Jordan read a message from O'Conner moments before the opening tip-off: "Let me wish you luck in tonight's game. You're playing a great team. We are all aware that Notre Dame has not beaten Indiana since 1946 and my only desire is to see you end this famine tonight. Go on out there and win this one for me. I'll be pulling for you all the way."

The Irish jumped to 41-28 halftime lead before fighting off a furious IU rally.

Against Kansas State, the Hoosiers lost when center Jack Carby hit a 40-foot shot with five seconds left. That gave Kansas State its 23rd straight home victory.

NEW RECORD Schlundt broke his own single-game mark by scoring 39 points in a 91-88 victory over Michigan. He would have five other games that season with more than 30 points.

HIGHLIGHTS Before a Fieldhouse record crowd of 10,056, IU beat Illinois 74-70 in two overtimes behind White's two free throws. The Hoosiers made six free throws in the second extra period. Schlundt finished with a team-high 22 points ... IU made a record 42 free throws and beat host Purdue 88-75. Schlundt was 16-for-20 from the line ... The Hoosiers defeated Butler 105-70 to break century mark for first time in school history. The win moved IU to second in the country behind unbeaten Seton Hall.

UNIMPRESSED COACH The Hoosiers, who had extended their victory streak to nine by beating Butler, were threatening to overtake Seton Hall. Its coach, John Russell, wasn't impressed.

"People think Indiana is playing a tougher schedule than ours," Russell told the wire service. "Nothing is further from the truth. It's just that Big Ten reputation. Big Ten basketball teams get by on the reputation built up in football."

McCracken had a different view.

"I would compare our schedule with any in the country. It's as tough as they come. As far as basketball living off the reputation of football, that just isn't true. This league has been producing good teams for a long, long time."

SCOTT IS LOST In February, backup center Lou Scott became academically ineligible. Without another true center on the roster, Schlundt's defensive intensity slipped.

"I play loose now," he told the Indianapolis Star. "There's nobody tall enough to come in and I have to avoid fouls. Branch had me change."

ANOTHER RECORD Schlundt scored 31 points in a 113-78 victory over Purdue. That gave him 822 for his career and broke Billy Garrett's school record.

Also, IU set a new school mark for most points in a game; and the teams combined for a Big Ten record 204 shots. They made 71.

CLINCH THE BIG TEN Dick Farley made a Big Ten-record eight of nine shots as the Hoosiers rolled to a 91-79 victory over Illinois to win their first undisputed conference title.

Players carried a jubilant McCracken off the floor on their shoulders.

"The boys did it," McCracken told The Champaign Urbana News Gazette. "They hustled all the way. They hustle in every game. Yes, in every practice. Give them the credit. I don't care if you don't mention my name."

"This is the greatest thing that's happened to me," said forward Charley Kraak. "I don't imagine Illinois can realize how badly we've wanted this one. They've had so many."

Champaign Urbana News Gazette sports editor Jack Prowell wrote afterward: "You can put it down in your little black book that Indiana is going to give any and all comers a rough time in the NCAA Tournament….There's no reason why Indiana can't go all the way."

A TIME TO PRAISE During a victory celebration the next day, the Indianapolis News reported McCracken's heart-felt words to his players:

"I never praise you fellows and sometimes you must think I'm pretty hard. I criticize and tell you where you do the wrong things, and leave the praise to your mothers and sweethearts and friends. But tonight I'll have to say that you're the greatest team in the country."

The 1953 Indiana Hoosiers won the school's first undisputed Big Ten Championship.

TOP OF THE HEAP The victory was IU's 16th in a row and boosted the Hoosiers to No. 1 for the first time in school history. Notre Dame athletic director Ed Krause sent McCracken the following telegram:

"Congratulations on being the No. 1 team in the nation. We all voted for you. However, remember, Notre Dame is still No. 1 in Indiana."

HOOSIERS UPSET A week later, on March 7, Minnesota upset IU 65-63 on a basket with three seconds left to end Indiana's 17-game win streak. The Hoosiers wouldn't lose again,

THE NCAA TOURNEY Indiana was the favorite to win the 22-team field, with No. 2 Washington picked second.

In the opening-round game in Chicago, Schlundt scored 23 points (14 in the final 15 minutes) and Leonard had 22 as IU edged DePaul 82-80.

That set up a rematch with Notre Dame. With Schlundt scoring a school-record 41 points (including 18 in the first 10 minutes), IU rolled to a 79-66 victory.

Indiana advanced to Kansas City and a semifinal showdown with Louisiana State and All-American center Bob Pettit. Schlundt and Leonard combined for 51 points as the hot-shooting Hoosiers, hitting 55 percent from the field, won 80-67. Pettit finished with 29 points.

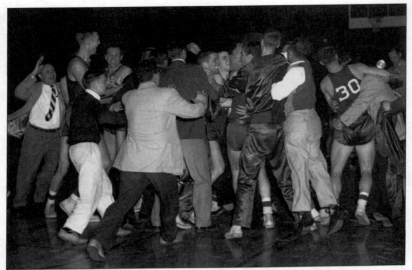

The Indiana Hoosiers celebrate winning the 1953 NCAA Championship in Kansas City.

TITLE REMATCH The Hoosiers met defending champion Kansas, the school they had beaten for the 1940 crown. IU won the tense, rugged game 69-68 on Leonard's free throw in the closing seconds.

"I wanted to make the shots as much as anything I've ever wanted in my life," Leonard told the Indianapolis Times. "In fact, I had to make them."

TIME TO PARTY A huge victory celebration followed in Bloomington. It featured Chicago sports personality (and later Chicago Cubs announcer) Jack Brickhouse as the guest speaker. McCracken told the crowd that "The boys were marvelous. I've never seen such spirit and determination. But the game could have gone either way."

McCracken also denied rumors he would retire, saying he would coach "As long as my heart holds out." A week later, the Indianapolis Alumni organization presented McCracken with a Lincoln Capri, at the time one of the nation's top luxury cars.

POSTSEASON HONORS Schlundt was unanimously voted the Big Ten's most valuable player and made All-American. McCracken was voted national coach of the year.

BETTER NEXT YEAR? With every starter returning, IU was favored to become the first team to win back-to-back national championships. Reporters asked McCracken if the Hoosiers could improve.

"I would think so," McCracken said in the Champaign Urbana News Gazette. "No basketball player stands still. He either gets better or gets worse. I imagine some of my boys will improve. If the right ones do, we'll be better off next year. But that's a long way off."

THE 1953-54 SEASON

IU was favored to win a second straight national championship. The Hoosiers were ranked No. 1 and won their first six games before losing at Oregon State, 67-51.

Indiana won nine straight (including a 71-63 victory at Minnesota before a crowd of 18,872, the largest ever to watch a game in a college-owned arena) en route to its second straight conference title with a 12-2 record. An 82-64 loss to Iowa snapped the Hoosiers' 22-game home-court winning streak.

But it all ended in Iowa City in the tournament's opening round, when Notre Dame upset IU 65-64. The Hoosiers had beaten the Irish 66-55 during the regular season.

"That was hard to take," White told Inside Indiana years later. "We had beaten Notre Dame soundly early in the season. But I can remember Schlundt and Leonard were held to something like 19 points combined.

"I remember Leonard was put back into the game for the last play and scored a layup for what looked like the winning points. But he was called for charging into Dick Rosenthal (now the Irish athletic director) and we lost a chance for a second straight title."

Added Leonard: "I drove for the layup and scored, but was called for charging. My points counted. But Rosenthal was given two free throws and he made them. That was the game.

"I'll never forget that loss. We had such a great team. Of course, Notre Dame was a basketball power then. They had an outstanding team, but we had beaten them in the regular season. I still feel we were the better team."

Don Schlundt scores two points in IU's win over LSU in an NCAA consolation game.

Indiana came back to win the consolation game over Louisiana State, 73-62, to finish with a 20-4 mark.

Leonard made Look Magazine's All-American first team. Schlundt, who averaged a team-high 24.3 points and set another record by scoring 47 points against Ohio State, was a second-team choice.

Look Magazine had this to say about Leonard in its March 9, 1954 issue:

"It is Leonard's feinting and pinpoint passing that set up so many of the scores for his more publicized, higher-scoring teammate, Schlundt. And Leonard himself is an outstanding set shot. Jim Enright, Big Ten officials, says 'The Hoosiers go as Leonard goes, Schlundt notwithstanding.' "

THE 1954-55 SEASON

Indiana, trying to become the first team to win three straight Big Ten titles since Chicago in 1908-10, returned only three mainstays in Schlundt, Burke Scott and Dick White.

Still, the Hoosiers were ranked fourth in preseason polls and picked as a conference favorite. McCracken wasn't so sure.

"We hope to finish somewhere in the first division, but those picking us among the top contenders simply aren't facing the facts," McCracken said.

Indiana proved him right by finishing 8-14, the worst record of his career. IU also lost four straight non-conference games for first time since 1930.

HIGHLIGHTS Indiana snapped Notre Dame's 22-game home win streak with a 73-70 victory. Sophomore Hallie Bryant came off bench to score 12 second-half points ... Schlundt scored 41 in an 83-78 loss to Southern Methodist ... In a 95-77 win over Michigan, the Hoosiers set a Big Ten record with 43 free throws ... The Hoosiers beat Purdue for the 13th consecutive time (a series record) with a 75-62 victory in Bloomington. They retained the Fire Bell trophy, symbolic of the rivalry. Wally Choice led IU with 29 points ... Purdue took back the Fire Bell for the first time since 1948 when it won the rematch 92-67 a week later in West Lafayette ... Choice finished strong to become the Hoosiers' second-leading scorer with a 14.4 average.

BREAKING THE BARRIER Schlundt became the first Big Ten player and just the sixth major college player to score 2,000 points when he got 20 in a 65-58 win over Wisconsin on Feb. 7, 1955. He finished the game with 2,017.

At that time, the leaders were Furman's Frank Selvy (2,538) and Loyola's Jim Lacy (2,154). The other 2,000-point scorers were Wake Forest's Dick Hemric, LaSalle's Tom Gola and John Carroll's George Dalton.

Since then, more than 300 NCAA Division I players have scored at least 2,000 points. The leader remains LSU's Pete Marovich, who scored the last of his 3,667 points in 1970.

Don Schlundt became the first player in Big Ten history to score over 2,000 career points.

BIG FINALE Schlundt ended his college career by scoring 47 points in an 84-66 victory over visiting Ohio State. That tied the conference record he'd set last year, also against Ohio State. He won All-American honors and was voted college basketball's player of the year.

Schlundt was picked in the NBA draft by defending champion

TRYING FOR WILT

Wilt Chamberlain twice visited the IU campus that season. The last came during the Hoosiers' 85-78 home loss to Northwestern.

That visit came two days after the high school senior from Philadelphia had scored 90 points in a game.

Indiana wasn't the only one interested in the heralded 7-1 center. The NBA, the Harlem Globetrotters and every major college were after him. He reportedly had been offered $12,000 to turn pro, a huge sum at the time.

Wilt Chamberlain

Chamberlain told the Indianapolis News in a Feb. 22 story that he hadn't made a decision and wouldn't until the spring. McCracken wasn't optimistic.

"Everybody in the country is after him. I don't think we have too good a chance to get him."

That spring, Chamberlain announced for Kansas.

Syracuse. He turned down an offer of $5,500 a year, plus a $1,000 bonus, to go into the insurance business.

THE 1955-56 SEASON

The Hoosiers were looking to bounce back with top returnees Wally Choice and Hallie Bryant, a former Mr. Basketball from Indianapolis Crispus Attucks.

McCracken also had an outstanding sophomore group that included Archie Dees, Ray Ball, Charley Brown, Pete Obremskey and Paxton Lumpkin.

The 6-8, 195-pound Dees was set to replace Schlundt.

With the sophomores getting plenty of action, IU opened 2-0 and jumped to 19th in the national poll. But the Hoosiers struggled after that, lost Brown and Lumpkin to academic ineligibility in the second semester, and finished 13-9 overall and 6-8 in the Big Ten.

A former Indiana Mr. Basketball, Hallie Bryant played for the Hoosiers before playing in the NBA and then joining the Harlem Globetrotters.

HIGHLIGHTS Bryant scored 31 in 80-61 win over Cincinnati..... Choice had 26 in 94-70 win over Butler.... Choice went 12-for-12 from the line in an 84-82 victory over Northwestern .... Choice shot 51 percent from the field to break Schlundt's season record of 50.5. He averaged a team-high 21.5 points. Dees was next at 17.4. He also averaged 12.6 rebounds. Bryant averaged 14.4 points. He led the Big Ten in free throw shooting at 88 percent.

Bryant went on to play 13 seasons with the Harlem Globetrotters after a brief stint in the NBA with the St. Louis Hawks.

IMPROVED SHOOTING In 1951, two players in the nation averaged better than 50 percent from field. The next year three players did it. The number increased to nine in 1953, 10 in '54, 15 in '55 and 17 in '56.

McCracken credited the jump shot, which started replacing the one-handed shot in the late 1940s.

"Tell me how you stop that shot?" he asked in an Indianapolis Star story. "The shooter puts the ball behind his head, away from the defensive man and shoots on a jump while falling away from the basket. All you can do is hope they don't go in."

THE 1956-57 SEASON

With eight lettermen and four returning starters, prospects were promising. McCracken called the team "the fastest since our 1951 club with considerably more size."

Indiana finished 14-8 overall. The Hoosiers went 10-4 in the Big Ten to share the title with Michigan State.

Dees started strong with 28 point-games in victories over Valparaiso and Southern Illinois. Ten days later, he scored 31 in a victory over LaSalle. His 25.4-point average led the Big Ten.

LATE BLOOMER Senior forward Dick Neal got hot in Big Ten play, starting with a 22-point effort in a victory over Michigan. After playing sparingly during the pre-conference season, he finished second on the team with a 15.6 average.

NEW RULES The NCAA made two major rules changes. 1) A team won't get into one-and-one situation until opponents have six fouls in a half (before one-and-ones started with the first foul). 2) The ball can't be tossed into the free throw area during an in-bound play from under the basket.

Archie Dees had back-to-back 28 point games to start the 1956-57 season.

ANOTHER INNOVATION During a 73-68 victory over Michigan, assistant coach Lou Watson went into the press area and made comments into a tape recorder. Besides doing some play-by-play, Watson pointed out mistakes and praised players. The players listened to the tape after the game. McCracken told the Indianapolis Star it was the first time he'd used the gimmick. He said it was intended to help players correct mistakes and improve their play.

HIGHLIGHTS In 79-68 win over Wisconsin, Dees had 28 points and 23 rebounds. Neal had 10 points and 26 rebounds … IU beat Minnesota 91-72 as Neal made 11-of-13 shots for 24 points. He added 10 rebounds. Dees had 29 points and 20 rebounds … Dees scored a career-high 37 in a 90-76 win over Iowa, then topped it with 39 points in an 87-76 loss to Michigan … Senior guard Clarence Doninger, now IU's athletic director, scored no points in limited action. He joined the team at midseason when injuries and academic difficulties left the team without enough players.

SCORING RECORD Illinois beat Indiana 112-91 to set a conference mark for most combined points. It was the Hoosiers' most points ever in loss. They came back to beat the Illini 84-76 and earn a share

Branch McCracken is carried off the floor after the Hoosiers won a share of the 1957 Big Ten Championship

of the conference crown with Michigan State.

BID GOES TO SPARTANS Michigan State got the NCAA Tournament bid because Big Ten rules stipulated that, in the event of a tie, it go to the team that hadn't participated the longest. The Spartans had never made it before.

THE 1957-58 SEASON

Indiana capped one of the most amazing turnarounds in Big Ten history by winning seven of its last eight games to capture the conference championship and qualify for the NCAA Tournament.

The Hoosiers opened the season 1-6, their worst start ever. That included a 76-68 loss to Ohio University, their first season-opening defeat in 29 years.

The only pre-conference bright spot came when Dees scored 62 points to set a Hoosier Classic record (the annual holiday event was held in Butler Fieldhouse and matched IU against Butler and Notre Dame). The Hoosiers still lost both games.

Indiana also struggled in Big Ten play. It opened 3-3, including a 68-66 loss to Purdue when Boilermaker forward Bob Fehrman scored with three seconds left off an offensive rebound. That spoiled Dees' 38-point effort.

THE TURNAROUND BEGINS IU started with a rough 82-79 victory over

Assistant coach Ernie Andres (left) and Branch McCracken.

Michigan State. The game included three fist fights (the most intense featured Michigan's 6-5 Larry Hedden squaring off against 6-1 Sam Gee) and a bench-clearing scuffle over a loose ball.

LET'S HAVE A TALK After a 93-87 win at Wisconsin, the Hoosiers play uninspired in a 93-83 loss to Ohio State. McCracken had a team meeting where he said, among other things, "What happened, boys, did you forget all the defensive basketball you've learned?"

In a rematch five days later, Dees scored 33 points as Indiana beat the Buckeyes 88-83.

HUGE COMEBACK The Hoosiers rallied from a 19-point deficit to win at Michigan, 95-88. They trailed 50-36 at halftime, which inspired another fiery McCracken talk.

"We had to get a few things straightened out," said McCracken.

Added guard Pete Obremskey: "We needed that talking to. I don't think we've ever been that lousy on defense. Man, 50 points. That's too many for any team to get on us in a half."

McCracken later called the victory "sheer guts and determination."

WINNER TAKE ALL Indiana and Michigan State met in the season finale to decide the Big Ten champion and NCAA participant. Both teams were tied with 9-4 conference marks.

The Hoosiers won 75-72 behind Bob Wilkinson's 18 points. Sam Gee added 17. IU got inspiration from Jerry Thompson, whose son was born the night before. Thompson scored 11 points.

NCAA TOURNEY IU opened with Notre Dame, which had beaten the Hoosiers 89-74 during the regular season. The Irish (24-4) won again, 94-87, behind Tom Hawkins' 31 points. Dees led Indiana with 28.

The Hoosiers won the consolation game over Miami of Ohio, 98-91.

Dees won his second straight Big Ten scoring title, with a 25.5 average. It was the fifth time in the last six years an IU player had done it. Dees became the first two-time Big Ten most valuable player and made the Look All-American team. His total of 1,546 points ranked second in conference history to Schlundt.

Archie Dees

"Archie is a great all-around basketball player who does everything well and never loses sight that he's part of the team," said McCracken.

Dees went on to play four years with the Cincinnati Royals. He later entered the insurance business with Schlundt.

Gee set a Big Ten mark by shooting 92 percent from the free throw line. The Hoosiers' 40-percent field goal shooting was a school record.

Still, it was the team performance McCracken pointed to.

"This team had as much courage and desire as any I've ever seen and it accomplished great things against tremendous odds. I hope the fans will remember it for its wonderful come-back to win the Big Ten and not measure it by the tournament performance.

"We were beaten in the tournament by a great team on one of its best nights. We neither offer nor need excuses, but those who saw us could see that we had lost our edge. A let-down just couldn't be avoided after the pressure, which kept mounting with every game in the last month."

That ended a six-year span during which the Hoosiers won four Big Ten titles, three undisputed, and one NCAA crown. It would be nine years before they would win another conference championship.

THE 1958-59 SEASON

IU's 11-11 overall record, 7-7 in the Big Ten, had fans grumbling about the "run-and-shoot" offense, the lack of defense and mistake-ridden play.

The criticism caused McCracken to address the team

"Our fast break system has got a lot of criticism lately. Maybe some of you feel the same way about it. But let me assure you, if the system doesn't work, it's because you and I have failed to make it work. There's nothing wrong with the system itself."

It didn't help when the Hoosiers lost to Illinois, 100-98. It was the most points IU had ever scored in a loss.

Tired of the anti-McCracken talk, Everett Dean defended his former player in a letter that appeared in a basketball program.

"Branch McCracken is a better coach today than at any time in his career," wrote Dean. "Our university is fortunate to have .... a man of Mac's stature in his profession."

BELLAMY ARRIVES The Hoosiers were boosted by 6-11 sophomore center Walt Bellamy. A native of North Carolina, he came to Indiana with the encouragement of his high school coach, who had done graduate work in Bloomington.

Bellamy had a strong season. He averaged 17.4 points and 15.2 rebounds. His 51.2 percent shooting from the field (mostly on dunks and layups) set a school record. That helped IU shoot a school record 40.7 percent from the field.

Walt Bellamy still holds Indiana's single game (33) and single season (428) rebounding records.

THE 1959-60 SEASON

McCracken and the Hoosiers came back with a vengeance. They won their final 12 games, whipped eventual national champion Ohio State by 16 points and started a push for sending more than one Big Ten team to the NCAA Tournament.

However, Indiana blew its chance to win the conference crown by losing its first three league games. The Hoosiers finished 20-4 and 11-3. Ohio State won the title with a 13-1 record.

With all five starters returning – Bellamy, Frank Radovich, LeRoy Johnson, Herbie Lee and Bob Wilkinson – McCracken told the Daily Student before the season the Hoosiers could be a "great club if they want to win bad enough."

The Hoosiers roared through the pre-conference schedule with an 8-1 record that included impressive victories over Kansas State, Notre Dame, Maryland and Louisville. The loss came at Missouri, 79-76, when Bellamy played just 14 minutes because of foul trouble.

BAD BEGINNING Ohio State was the only Big Ten team expected to challenge IU, but Purdue pulled off the huge upset in the league opener. The Boilermakers combined patient offense with a smothering zone defense that held Bellamy to eight points in a 79-76 win.

Northwestern followed the same formula in a 61-57 victory two days later. The Wildcats spread their offense and had their guards pass the ball back and forth until Bellamy and Radovich moved away from the basket. Then the guards drove for layups or passed off for easy buckets.

A frustrated McCracken had enough.

"This is not basketball," he told the Indianapolis Star. "I can understand it when a team plays a patterned offense. But this kind of stuff is simply stalling around.

"I'm going to call for the 24-second rule at our next coaches' meeting. No one should have to foul to be able to get a shot during a two-minute period of play."

HERE COME THE BUCKEYES With a sophomore class that featured Jerry Lucas and John Havlicek, Ohio State was projected as the team of the future. That future became the present when IU threw the ball away twice in the final minute, blew a 95-91 lead and lost 96-95 when guard Larry Siegfried scored with five seconds left.

Havlicek led the Buckeyes with 21 points. Reserve guard Bob Knight scored one point during Ohio State's late rally. Herbie Lee led IU with 23 points.

"Man, oh man, oh man," said McCracken in the Indianapolis Star. "Did you ever see kids play their hearts out as much as ours did today and then make three or four silly mistakes the last couple of minutes and lose?

"They (Ohio State) can't say they won. We gave it to 'em. We had it won and simply kicked it away."

TIME FOR A CHANGE McCracken switched to a zone defense even though he had always preferred man-to-man. The result – Indiana didn't lose again.

"I probably shouldn't say I dislike the zone," said McCracken said after the streak had reached six. "The boys are doing a good job with it and its getting the job done."

THE OHIO STATE REMATCH Just before the game, IU officials suspended Lee for unspecified school violations. He was averaging 10.7 points.

But it would take more than that to stop the Hoosiers. Wilkinson expressed everyone's feelings when he spoke the morning of the game to a Daily Student reporter.

"We can't make up for a whole season in one game, but we're going to beat them tonight and perhaps make up for that game we handed them earlier in the season."

IU jumped to a 23-10 lead and never looked back in a 99-83 victory. Bellamy scored 24 points. Wilkinson added 21. The Hoosiers shot 53 percent from the field.

"There wasn't a thing we could do," said Ohio State coach Fred Taylor. "They were just a much better club than we."

It was Ohio State's only conference loss. In the final wire service poll, the Buckeyes were ranked third. IU was ranked 10.

Late in his coaching career, Branch McCracken was criticized for his up-tempo style of play.

TAKING THE BLAME During the awards banquet after the season, McCracken told a large crowd that "This bunch of boys could beat anyone in the country. I'd love to walk out of here and play in the NCAA....

"It's probably my fault we lost those three games. I had the boys too high for some of the non-conference games. Sometimes it does you good to lose a game or two early in the season."

McCracken later added the slow start was caused by "Too much publicity. We won the tournaments at Indianapolis and Louisville, and we were getting all those write-ups. The players came home with gold watches and they didn't come down to earth until they lost."

WRAPUP Bellamy led team in scoring (22.4) and rebounding (13.5). He scored a career high 42 points in a 92-78 win over Illinois. Radovich was next at 14.8 points and 11.9 rebounds. The Hoosiers averaged a school-record 83.3 points.

RADIO DEBUT One of the radio announcers for IU games was Dick Enberg, then a student at Indiana. He would later find national success at NBC.

OLYMPIC BOUND Bellamy was one of 12 players picked for the U.S. Olympic team that won a 1960 gold medal in Rome.

Bellamy's selection came after his all-star team – which also featured Oscar Robertson and Jerry West – won the eight-team NCAA University tourney. He scored 42 points in the three games.

THE 1960-61 SEASON

With Bellamy returning for his senior year, McCracken was optimistic.

"This boy has improved more in three years than anyone I've ever

The 1960 U.S. Olympic team featured Walt Bellamy (back row, third from left) of Indiana, along with Ohio State's Jerry Lucas (back row, second from left) and future NBA stars Jerry West (second row, second from right) and Oscar Robertson (back row, far right).

had," said McCracken. "This should be his greatest year."

Bellamy averaged 21.8 points and 17.8 rebounds and won All-American honors. He became IU's career leader with 1,088 rebounds, a record that lasted until 1995, when Alan Henderson finished with 1,091.

The Hoosiers appeared to have plenty of fire power from their sophomore class. There was Tom Bolyard, who averaged 30 points as a high school senior in Fort Wayne. Jimmy Rayl had averaged 30 points and become Mr. Basketball during a standout career at Kokomo. New Castle's Ray Pavy, who as a senior finished second in the state in scoring to Rayl and was part of the most memorable shoot-out in Indiana high school history (in a game against Kokomo, Pavy scored 51 points to Rayl 's 49), was also ready.

Bolyard had the biggest impact. He averaged 15.5 points and 9.0 rebounds. Pavy became a frequent starter at point guard, averaging 2.5 points. Rayl averaged 4.1 points, but shot just 30.4 percent from the field.

The Hoosiers were playing in the new Fieldhouse, which was to be a temporary home until Assembly Hall was built. Expected to be just a few seasons, it lasted 11.

High-scoring Tom Bolyard came to Bloomington from Fort Wayne, Ind.

HIGHLIGHTS Indiana debuted the Fieldhouse with an 80-53 victory over Indiana State before 9,236 fans..... McCracken got his 300th victory at IU in a 74-69 win over Notre Dame at Fort Wayne's Memorial Coliseum..... Bellamy had 22 points and 18 rebounds in a 93-82 win over visiting Illinois. It was McCracken's 400th career victory..... In an 82-67 win over Michigan, Bellamy had 28 points and a Big Ten-record 33 rebounds. The Hoosiers had 95 rebounds to set a conference record that still stands.

A mid-season slump cost Indiana a shot at the Big Ten crown. The Hoosiers finished 15-9 and 8-6. Ohio State repeated as champion.

ON TO THE NBA Chicago picked Bellamy in the first round. He became the 1962 rookie of the year. He later played for Baltimore, New York, Detroit, Atlanta and New Orleans. During a 13-year career, he averaged 20.1 points and 13.6 rebounds. He finished with 20,941 points and was elected to the Basketball Hall of Fame.

THE 1961-62 SEASON

Tragedy struck the Hoosiers in the fall, when Pavy was involved in a car accident. Pavy's fiancee was killed. His back was broken in three places and his spinal cord was irreparably damaged. He would never walk again.

Pavy returned to school and graduated in 1964. He later became the head basketball coach at Sulphur Springs and Shenandoah, then moved on as an administrator in the New Castle Community School Corporation. He was inducted into Indiana Basketball Hall of Fame in 1990. After Landon Turner was paralyzed in a 1981 car accident, Bob Knight sought Pavy's advice on buying a van and living accommodations.

Ray Pavy's career was ended abruptly when his spinal cord was damaged in a tragic car accident.

BACK TO THE FIREWAGON Without Bellamy, the Hoosiers lacked inside size. McCracken compensated with up-tempo play.

"We sort of drifted away from the firewagon game with the good big men we've had in the last 10 years," he said in the media guide. "Now we intend to go back to it and be a running club. We've played the other fellows' game long enough .... We may throw the ball away a few times, but we'll have to forget that and keep running."

The running style produced the best offense, and worst defense, in school history. IU averaged 87 points a game while allowing 88.

BAD DEFENSE Five teams scored more than 100 points against Indiana. Seven others scored more than 90. The Hoosiers scored 100 against Minnesota and lost by four. They scored 94 against Wisconsin and lost by 11.

LOT OF POINTS Indiana tied its own school and conference record for points in a 122-95 victory over Notre Dame at Fort Wayne. The point total is still an IU record.

THE SPLENDID SPLINTER Rayl scored a conference-record 56 points in a 105-104 overtime win against Minnesota. His 20-foot jumper with two seconds left won it. His 20 field goals were another record.

After that game, McCracken called Rayl "the greatest shooter in the game today."

Rayl rebounded from a poor sophomore season with a school-record 29.8 scoring average. George McGinnis broke it in 1971 with a 29.9 average.

Rayl also set conference marks by going 15-for-15 from the line against Michigan and making 32 straight free throws.

Rayl, known as the Splendid Splinter because of his 6-1, 145-pound frame, told Inside Indiana in 1995 that he liked the Hurryin' Hoosiers' style.

"I took a lot of shots at IU, but that was the way we played the game. Everybody got a lot of shots. I would get 25-30 shots and Bolyard would get 18-20. There's not that many shots to go around these days."

Bolyard averaged 18.6 points and 9.5 rebounds.

With IU stumbling to 13-11 and 7-7, critics turned harsh. McCracken remembered the criticism years later in an interview with the Indianapolis Star.

"When my boys were taking a pretty good pasting, I heard rumors of 'McCracken's too old,' " he said. "I couldn't help thinking back to the 1939 season when I wished I could add a few years. I guess whether you're 30 or 50, it's just the right age as long as you're winning ball games."

Jimmy Rayl twice scored 56 points in a game to set an IU record that still stands today.

THE 1962-63 SEASON

The Hoosiers had a good group of sophomores with 6-4 twins Tom and Dick VanArsdale, plus 6-5 Jon McGlocklin.

The VanArsdales had been co-Mr. Basketballs for Indianapolis Manual High School.

With the weakness again at center, McCracken looked to push the pace while improving the defense.

"We've got speed to burn and we intend to use it," he said in the media guide. "We'll fastbreak whenever we can.

"On defense, we can't help but be stronger. I've seen enough ability out there to convince me we aren't going to give up points like we did last year."

He was right. The Hoosiers allowed 84 points a game while scoring at an 84.7 clip.

STILL HOT Rayl continued his phenomenal scoring. With a range approaching 30 feet, his shots often left opponents shaking their heads.

"I shot 48 times one night," said Rayl. "In some games today, the entire Indiana team is lucky to shoot 48 times.

"Branch was pretty good about it. I took a lot of bad shots. There's no question about that. But Branch never said much about it."

ANOTHER 56 Rayl tied his record in a 113-94 win over Michigan State. He scored that many despite missing seven straight open jumpers

Rayl told Inside Indiana in 1995 that "If I'd hit half of those, I would have had a really great game.

"A lot of coaches would have taken a player out if he missed seven straight. That never entered my mind. I kept right on going and pretty soon I was back hitting the shots."

WRAPPING IT UP Rayl again led the team with a 25.3 average, although he shot just 41.7 percent from the field. Bolyard averaged 20 points and 7.2 rebounds.

The VanArsdales made a big impact. Tom averaged 12.5 points and 9.3 rebounds. Dick averaged 12.2 points and 8.9 rebounds.

Jimmy Rayl led the Hoosiers in scoring two consecutive years and was named an All-American.

Rayl made All-American. He finished fourth on IU's career scoring with 1,401 points behind Don Schlundt, Archie Dees and Walt Bellamy. He now ranks 15th.

Rayl later played two seasons for the Indiana Pacers in the American Basketball Association before becoming a sales rep with the Xerox Corporation.

Bolyard finished fifth on IU scoring lists with 1,299 points. He now ranks 18th. He became an assistant coach under Lou Watson before moving on to the IU Alumni Association.

THE 1963-64 SEASON

The Hoosiers couldn't make up for the loss of Rayl and Bolyard. They suffered through an eight-game losing streak and losses in 11 of 12 games, the worst drought of McCracken's career.

With the defense continuing to allow scoreboard-breaking totals, criticism hit a peak. On his way to a 9-15 record, McCracken had this to say to a group of sportswriters in Chicago:

"The kind of job I want would be coach of an orphanage, where there are no parents to come around, or at a state penitentiary, where the alumni never come back."

Stress took its toll during the eight-game losing streak. Jack Schneider, a sports writer for The Louisville Times, wrote an open letter advising McCracken to retire for his well being.

Identical twins Tom (#25) and Dick (#30) VanArsdale finished their Indiana careers with nearly identical stats.

"I realize basketball has been practically your entire life, from your days as a star player at Monrovia High School and Indiana U. and continuing through your distinguished 31-year coaching career. But is it worth all this anguish and torment? It can't be. You're 56 years old, Mac, with a lot of good living ahead of you, if your health holds out. I wonder how long it can if the strain you have experienced the last few weeks goes on much longer."

BRIGHT SPOTS Dick VanArsdale led the team in scoring (22.3) and rebounding (12.5) Tom VanArsdale was next at 21.3 and 12.4. The only other Hoosier to score in double figures was Jon McGlockin at 15.7.

Indiana scored at an 84.7 clip while allowing 83.9 points.

THE FINAL SEASON

The Hoosiers returned to Big Ten title contention. They won their first nine games, including a 107-81 victory over North Carolina before a Fieldhouse-record crowd of 10,301.

After losing their Big Ten opener to Illinois, they won six of their next seven to take sole possession of second place behind Michigan. A 96-95 overtime loss to the Wolverines at the Fieldhouse cost them a shot at the title and an NCAA Tournament berth.

IU finished 19-5 and 9-5. Michigan won the league crown with a 13-1 mark.

LEADING THE WAY Tom VanArsdale averaged 18.4 points and 8.6 rebounds. Dick VanArsdale averaged 17.2 and 8.7.

They finished their careers with almost identical numbers. Tom

The Hoosiers of 1964-65 were the last to be coached by Branch McCracken.
Assistant coach Lou Watson (second row, far left) took over the next season.

totaled 1,252 points and 723 rebounds. Dick had 1,240 points and 719 rebounds.

They were NBA second-round picks: Tom to Detroit, Dick to Phoenix. Both played 12 seasons. Dick averaged 16.4 points. Tom averaged 15.3.

Dick later became the TV color commentator of Phoenix games. In 1987, he became the Suns' interim coach when John MacLeod was fired.

REACHING THE END Two weeks after the season, with a career record of 457-215, McCracken knew more than a quarter-century of coaching was over. He submitted a brief letter of resignation:

"My association with Indiana University as a student, player and coach has been a long and rewarding one. I am sincerely grateful to those alumni, friends, faculty, administrators, coaches – and especially to those fine young men who have played for me – for giving me the opportunity to serve Indiana University as head basketball coach to the best of my ability.

"However, I feel that I must now submit my resignation and request I be relieved of my duties in accordance with the terms of my contract."

A Herald-Telephone editorial on Mac's retirement stated, "We know there will be other bright spots for the Hurryin' Hoosiers because our state knows no peer in the development of superior hoopsters. Like Stan Musial, Red Grange or Jack Dempsey, however, it will take super efforts on the parts of future IU coaches to match the record of "The Big Bear", "The Sheriff", "The Pride of Monrovia.""

On June 4, 1970, Branch McCracken died of a heart ailment. He was 61.

The Lou Watson- Jerry Oliver Years

The search for McCracken's replacement didn't take long. Less than a month after the season, 41-year-old IU assistant coach Lou Watson signed a three-year contract.

Watson was chosen ahead of such candidates as Louisiana State Coach Jay Creary, future Indiana Pacers Coach Bob Leonard, Indianapolis Broad Ripple Coach Gene Ring and Columbus High School Coach Bill Stearman. All were former IU players.

"This is something I've always dreamed of," said Watson. "I know it's not going to be easy. It won't be easy following Mac. He's a great institution in himself."

After playing for McCracken in the late 1940s and early 1950s, Watson turned down an $8,500 offer to play professional basketball for the Chicago Stags to become an IU assistant. He spent three years at Huntington (Ind.) High School before returning to Indiana in 1955.

Said McCracken, who had recommended Watson for the job: "I'm tickled to death the university has selected Lou. He's a fine young coach and will do an excellent job."

There were no guarantees. The Hoosiers lost their top seven scorers from the previous season. Only 148 points returned from a squad that scored 2,018.

Indiana Coach Lou Watson (center) with assistant coach Jerry Oliver (right) and fresh-man coach Tom Bolyard (left).

ROUGH DEBUT The Hoosiers struggled to an 8-16 record. They were last in the Big Ten with a 4-10 record.

However, there were hopeful signs. IU lost three games by one point. The Hoosiers beat Michigan State near the end of the season to deny the Spartans the conference championship.

Guard Max Walker averaged a team-high 16.5 points.

THE 1966-67 SEASON

Picked to finish fifth in the Big Ten, Indiana surprised everybody by sharing the co-championship with Michigan State (becoming the first Big Ten team to go from last to first in consecutive seasons) and qualifying for its first NCAA Tournament since 1958.

"We won because everybody put the team ahead of himself," said Watson. "We worked together and got the ball to the open man."

IU finished 18-8 overall and 10-4 in the Big Ten. A six-game winning streak early in the conference season boosted the Hoosiers to the top of the standings and they stayed there the rest of the way.

Forward Butch Joyner was an All-Big Ten choice after averaging 18.5 points and 10.5 rebounds. He shot 50.1 percent from the field.

Guard Vernon Payne averaged 15.7 points and made the Small-American (under 6-foot) team.

NCAA TOURNEY Despite having four players score in double figures, IU lost to Virginia Tech 79-70. In the consolation game, the Hoosiers beat Tennessee 51-44 behind center Bill DeHeer's 13 points.

Harry (Butch) Joyner made the All-Big Ten team after averaging double figures in points and rebounds for the Hoosiers.

THE 1967-69 SEASONS

Indiana had consecutive last-place conference finishes. The Hoosiers went 10-14 and 9-15. Joyner again made All-Big Ten honors in 1968 after averaging 13.9 points and 8.3 rebounds. In 1969, guard Joe Cooke was the leading scorer with a 21.8 average. Forward Kenny Johnson averaged 18.2 points and 12.1 rebounds.

The good news came from recruiting. Newcomers included sophomore Joby Wright and freshmen John Ritter and Frank

Kenny Johnson pulled down an average of 12 rebounds while scoring over 18 points a game for the 1969 Hoosiers.

Wilson. All would contribute to IU's future success.

THE 1969-70 SEASON

That fall, Watson herniated a disc in his back. He had surgery and missed the entire 1969-70 season. He was replaced by assistant coach Jerry Oliver.

Oliver arrived at IU in 1968 after a successful tenure at Indianapolis Washington High School. His eight-year record was 162-36. That included the 1965 state championship.

Oliver's success and expertise with a pressing defense contributed to his hiring. It didn't hurt that two of his Washington players – George McGinnis and Steve Downing – were among the state's best.

In fact, in 1969, McGinnis, Downing and new coach Bill Green led the Continentals to an unbeaten state championship. The next year, both players went to Indiana.

After taking over for Watson, Oliver endured a 7-17 record and another last-place finish. IU was hurt when leading scorer Joe Cooke

Joby Wright goes up for two points in a game against Ball State in 1969.

(22.3 average after 12 games) became ineligible for the second semester.

However, sophomore Joby Wright averaged 14.7 points and 8.4 rebounds. With McGinnis and Downing set to play the next season, prospects appeared bright.

THE 1970-71 SEASON

Watson was fully recovered. He said he was ready to turn the Hoosiers around.

"After sitting out last season with an ailing back, I'm happy to be mended and back at the job and more than anxious to get the season under way."

Expectations were high. McGinnis and Downing looked strong; Wright and James Harris were back. Big Ten championship fever was high, boosted even more by the football team's dismal 1-9 performance.

Disappointment followed. An early loss at Michigan was followed two weeks later by an 85-81 home defeat to Purdue. Fans, restless

George McGinnis was an All-American at Indiana in 1971 and went on to become a three-time NBA All-Star.

after three straight last-place finishes, became incensed.

Watson was barraged with hate mail. Boos and angry words followed his pre-game introductions. More and more empty seats appeared at The Fieldhouse (IU averaged 8,600 a game, almost 2,000 less than capacity).

Still, the Hoosiers won. Behind McGinnis, the eventual Big Ten leader in scoring (29.9) and rebounding (16.8), IU was the league's most high-powered team. A six-game winning streak gave the Hoosiers a 16-4 record heading into March. They still had a chance at the NCAA Tournament and the NIT.

NCAA hopes ended with a 94-87 overtime loss at Wisconsin. During IU's next game, a 104-88 victory over Iowa at The Fieldhouse, anti-Watson student signs appeared. Afterward, Watson suggested he would resign if he didn't have the team's support.

A series of secret players' meetings followed. They brought in Dr. John Brown, a professor of Urban Education who was close to some of the players.

Reported problems included lack of communication, favoritism toward some players (McGinnis and guard John Ritter), violation of some players' human rights (not racial), lack of discipline and a charge of just not learning basketball. The last issue was the players' biggest concern. At no time, they insisted, did they demand Watson's resignation.

After a 91-75 loss at Ohio State, Brown presented the concerns to Watson, who then called athletic director Bill Orwig.

Finally, IU President John Ryan met with players, Orwig, faculty representatives, Brown and Watson. It was then that Watson resigned "for the best interest of the team, the university and my family." It was three days before the season finale against Illinois. Oliver would coach the last game.

Watson, who was hurt by the secret meetings and accusations, said, "I had been contemplating resigning since early fall, but I was anxious to go through this season with the squad because I was confident I could step out a winner.

"....I am proud of my 22 years at IU as a player and a coach.... I will do all in my power to help my successor and wish him and each member of the squad every success."

Ritter, the only player to support Watson, was so upset by the situation that he threatened to sit out the Illinois game.

"I think the players were completely wrong," he told The Louisville Courier-Journal & Times. "Too many of them have their

The 1971 Indiana Hoosiers. The last team to be coached by Lou Watson.

own selfish interests in mind. Rather than working hard, they blamed someone else. And about this communication thing: I always found Coach Watson's door open."

McGinnis said he knew of no favoritism.

"Coach Watson may have done things for me, but he did little things for everybody and I don't call that playing favorites," McGinnis told The Courier-Journal & Times. "I earned my starting job and I don't think anyone on the bench did enough to take it away."

Ritter did play against Illinois, which beat Indiana 103-87. The Hoosiers finished 17-7 and 9-5 and received no postseason bid.

Wright was the second-leading scorer with a 17.6 average. Harris averaged 12.1. Downing averaged 9.6 points and 9.1 rebounds.

Watson was reassigned in the athletic department. He eventually became an associate athletic director. He retired in 1987. Three years later, he was inducted into the Indiana University Athletic Hall of Fame.

Associate Athletic Director Lou Watson.

THE SEARCH BEGINS Orwig began searching for a new coach immediately. Many believed it would be someone of national renown.

"We will be looking around the country at the outstanding coaches," said Orwig, "and we want the new man as quickly as we can get him because of the urgency of recruiting."

Orwig said Oliver would get consideration and "won't be over-

IU Athletic Director Bill Orwig (left) introduces the Hoosiers "coach for infinity," Bob Knight, at a 1971 news conference.

looked."

Some wanted a black coach.

"I have no qualms about hiring a black coach if he is the man most qualified for the position," said Orwig.

Orwig was one of four men on the search committee. The others were professors Edwin Cady and Schuyler F. Otteson, and Indianapolis alumni leader William T. Smith.

The committee wanted someone who stressed defense and discipline; someone who could return IU to its national championship-winning ways.

In less than three weeks, they'd found their man. At a press conference, Orwig introduced him as "our coach for infinity."

Robert Montgomery Knight.

Title Games

A PERFECT SEASON

The halftime buzzer sounded and Bob Knight glanced at the scoreboard. With 20 minutes left in this 1976 national championship game, the top-ranked and unbeaten Hoosiers were in trouble.

Behind forward Rickey Green's inspired play, Michigan led 35-29. The Wolverines were not the opponent Indiana wanted to face. The Hoosiers had won two earlier thrillers, 80-74 in Ann Arbor and 72-67 in overtime at Assembly Hall.

Now they were in Philadelphia, a neutral site, bigger stakes. Could they do it one more time? Could they do it without starting guard Bobby Wilkerson, their best athlete and defender, who was in a Philadelphia hospital after suffering a concussion just three minutes into the game?

Knight had watched his motion offense misfire, botching layups, blowing opportunities.

"We figured out at halftime we must have missed seven or eight," said Knight after the game.

Enter Kent Benson.

IU's 6-foot-11 junior center had a solid first half with 10 points and three rebounds. Knight wanted more.

"We wanted to get the ball to Benson," said Knight. "We decided to increase the pressure defensively and go to a different phase of our offense with Benson staying inside instead of sliding out."

The adjustments paid off. Benson had 15 points and six rebounds in the second half. Indiana shot 60 percent from the field and made 21-of-27 free throws. The defense shut down Michigan.

The Hoosiers outscored the Wolverines 57-33 in the last 20 minutes and rolled to an 86-68 victory. It was their first national champi-

The 1976 Indiana Hoosiers, the last team to go undefeated and win the NCAA Championship.

The seniors from the 1976 IU team show off their trophies from that season. The seniors were (from left to right) Bobby Wilkerson, Tom Abernathy, Scott May, Jim Crews and Quinn Buckner.

onship since 1953 and – combined with a 65-51 semifinal win over UCLA – marked the end of the Bruins' dynasty.

"I don't know what I could have done to change the game," said Michigan coach Johnny Orr. "They made all those free throws when they had to make them and that's why they're the champions."

All-American forward Scott May, forward Tom Abernathy and guard Jim Crews were a combined 11-for-11 from the line.

May ended his college career with 26 points and eight rebounds. Benson had 25 and nine. Guard Quinn Buckner added 16 points and eight rebounds. Abernathy scored 11 points.

"This has been a two-year quest to get this thing done," says Knight, remembering the previous year's bitter 92-90 loss to Kentucky in the NCAA regional finals. "Last year I felt we were the best team in the country, but we just didn't get it put together. We were struggling a little when May broke his arm and I felt that this year that our advantage going into the tournament was that we had a set team."

The 35-year-old Knight, already in his 11th year of coaching, was asked what the championship meant.

"You know, this is a goal of every coach. It's almost beyond comprehension to realize you have the chance to do it. Maybe it will come to me tomorrow."

Tomorrow wasn't a day of rest for Knight. He had recruiting plans.

"I have train reservations to Washington to see a (high school) all-star game," he said. "They pay me well at Indiana and they're not paying me to relax."

THE SHOT

It is March 30, 1987, and Indiana's national championship hopes rest on one final possession.

The Hoosiers trail Syracuse 73-72. The clock ticks toward zero. The New Orleans Super Dome crowd of 64,959, which has already seen 13 ties and 19 lead changes, roars from its feet.

IU looks to get the ball to All-American guard Steve Alford, whose game-high 23 points include 7-for-10 shooting from 3-point range. But he is covered by Howard Triche.

Guard Keith Smart has the ball. He penetrates and passes to center Daryl Thomas, who has 20 points and seven rebounds. Thomas is just six feet from the basket, but under heavy defensive pressure from Syracuse's Derrick Coleman.

Thomas could force up a shot and hope. Maybe it would go in. Maybe he would be fouled. But four years with Knight have taught him to try another option.

Indiana's Keith Smart goes up for two points against Syracuse's Howard Triche in the 1987 NCAA Championship game.

Todd Meier (left), Daryl Thomas (center) and Steve Alford (right) celebrate IU's 1987 NCAA Championship.

"I saw that Coleman didn't take my fake," says Thomas after the game. "I spotted Keith in the corner and got the ball to him."

Smart is under defensive pressure himself, but he has the quickness and leaping ability to beat it. He soars into the air, angling toward the baseline and the corner while twisting to get off the shot. Swish. IU wins its fifth national championship.

"I want to thank Daryl for not taking his shot and passing the ball back to me," says Smart with a laugh. "That was a good decision on his part. But any one of my teammates could have made that shot."

A reporter asks Smart if he had ever made a bigger shot.

"Oh yes," says Smart, "in pick-up games."

Syracuse coach Jim Boeheim says his box-and-one defense was designed to shut down Alford.

"We didn't want Alford to beat us, but Smart broke loose at the end.

"My kids did everything I asked them to do. It boiled down to somebody making a big play at the end and Indiana did it."

Smart finishes strong. He scores 12 of IU's last 15 points as the Hoosiers rally from an eight-point deficit in the final minutes. He totals 21 points and is named the tournament's most valuable player. Not bad for someone who was flipping burgers just a few years before.

HOOSIER AVALANCHE

Six years after its unbeaten run, Indiana looked to once again find Philadelphia magic, its fourth national championship and second under Knight.

Basketball wasn't the dominant issue on this March 30, 1981 night. President Ronald Reagan was undergoing surgery following an assassination attempt earlier in the day. No one knew if he would survive. The NCAA Tournament committee waited until less than an hour before tip-off before deciding to play the game.

The Hoosiers came in on a roll unseen since UCLA's glory days. They had wiped out their previous four opponents by an average margin of 22.6 points.

Now they faced a North Carolina team that boasted future NBA stars James Worthy and Sam Perkins, plus a red-hot Al Wood, whose 39 points destroyed Virginia in the semifinals.

They also faced a hostile Louisiana State crowd still angry over Knight's celebrated run-in with an LSU fan following the 67-49 semi-final win over the Tigers. The fan confronted Knight in a hotel lobby after the game. Knight, lacking Job's patience, put him up against a wall and, legend says, deposited him in a garbage can. The incident generated national headlines.

The championship game was close for a half. IU led 27-26 thanks to guard Randy Wittman's outside shooting.

Then guard Isiah Thomas caught fire. Just moments into the second half, he converts two steals into layups. The lead quickly swells to 11.

Indiana's Ray Tolbert hoists an NCAA seal in celebration of the Hoosiers victory over North Carolina in the 1981 NCAA Championship game.

"Isiah is our catalyst," said Indiana center Ray Tolbert. "He makes us roll."

Added Knight: "The key for us were the two quick steals by Isiah. That got us going."

Late in the game, Knight went to a spread offense and the Tar Heels were forced to foul. The Hoosiers made 12 of 15 free throws in the final three minutes of a 63-50 victory. It was their closest game of the tournament.

Thomas scored 19 second-half points and finished with 23. He was named the tournament's most valuable player. Wittman had 16 points. Forward Landon Turner had 12 points and six rebounds.

North Carolina, which shot just 39 percent from the field in the second half, was led by Wood's 18 points. Worthy was held to seven.

"Indiana played as good a second half as anyone has against us this year," said North Carolina coach Dean Smith. "Isiah took over. His two steals at the start of the second half were devastating."

The national title capped a remarkable comeback for the Hoosiers, who started the season 7-5. They won their last 10 games and finished 26-9. At the time, it was the most losses ever by an NCAA champion. Since then, North Carolina State (26-10) in 1983, Villanova (25-10) in 1985 and Kansas (27-11) in 1988, have had worse records.

"I don't know how many times I heard or read where Isiah kept saying this team would improve," said Knight. "This group never lost sight of the fact that they could hang in there and win the Big Ten and get here. This is a tremendous credit to their perseverance."

SLICK UNDER PRESSURE

It was March 18, 1953, and Indiana guard Bob Leonard faced the most pressure-packed free throw of his life.

The Hoosiers were tied with Kansas, 68-68, with 27 seconds left in the championship game at Kansas City.

There already had been 10 lead changes and 14 ties. Neither team had led by more than six points. The biggest lead in the second half was three.

Leonard missed his first free throw attempt. But the senior guard and two-time All-American made his second. Kansas called time out.

Legendary Jayhawks coach Phog Allen set up a final play. His preference would have been to get the ball to All-American center B.H. Born, whose 26 points and 15 rebounds earned him tournament most valuable player honors. But Born had fouled out and Allen had to improvise.

The ball wound up in the hands of back-up center Jerry Alberts, who replaced Born. Alberts bricked a shot, the Hoosiers got the rebound and won their second national championship.

"That was the greatest thrill I've ever had," said Dick White, IU's sixth man.

Center Don Schlundt led IU with 30 points and 10 rebounds. Charley Kraak added 17 points and 13 rebounds. Leonard, who averaged more than 20 points in four NCAA tourney games, finished with 12.

Dick Farley of Indiana goes up for two points as IU's Dick White (#41) watches in the 1953 NCAA Title game against Kansas.

The game was full of emotion. The Hoosiers, playing in front of a pro-Kansas crowd, were called for three technical fouls. Some reports had them going to Schlundt, Leonard and Kraack. Others had Coach Branch McCracken getting at least one.

Late in the game, an irate McCracken screamed at the scorer's table that "You had five on him and you changed it to four. We're your guests and you're robbing us," after officials first ruled that Born had committed his fifth foul, then reversed themselves and said it was only four (reporters covering the game also had Born with only four fouls). Born fouled out for good a few minutes later.

Kansas Coach Phog Allen said the botched foul keeping was nothing new at Municipal Stadium.

"That mistake on Born's fouls brought on a bad situation and its not the first time it's happened here," Allen said. "They should get some new blood in here. They make mistakes all the time. It's time to quit doing things like they did 30 years ago."

Referee Al Lightner remembered McCracken's actions in a 1970 column that appeared in the Oregon Statesman:

"Along came the 1953 national championship at Kansas City..... We were there, with whistle. So was big Branch, with mouth. The natural collision occurred. During the course of the close, exciting contest, he was nailed with two technical fouls for vehemently disputing our calls. Fortunately for him and Indiana, Kansas failed to take advantage.

"We ran into McCracken the next morning in a hotel restaurant. He approached and spoke. This is when we knew what kind of man he was.

" 'I guess I gave you a pretty bad time last night,' he said. 'But I want you to know I'm that way during games and mean nothing personal by it. I hope you understand.'

"We did."

Indiana (23-3) finished with victories in 22 of its last 23 games. Its losses were all on the road: by one point to Notre Dame and by two to Kansas State and Minnesota. The Minnesota loss prevented the Hoosiers from becoming the first Big Ten team to go 18-0 in conference play.

"Those were fantastic times," said White. "I was part of an outstanding team."

THE BOYS GO TO IT

It was March 29, 1940, the night before the title game between Indiana and Kansas in Kansas City. McCracken relaxed in a hotel room with Everett Dean. The coaches were talking strategy for the next day's game and Dean, whose Stanford team had lost to Kansas during the season, told McCracken to full-court press.

"If you let crack shots like Ebling, Allen, Hogben and Engleman roam free back of that foul ring, the Kansas half of the scoreboard will be busier than a hound dog in hunting season," said Dean.

McCracken took the advice.

"We played an all-floor defense," McCracken said. "We pressed them the moment the ball changed hands. It took stamina and conditioning, but it wrecked Kansas' set shots, let us play our fire-ball game and made us winners of the tournament."

With Marv Huffman and Jay McCreary scoring 12 points each, the Hoosiers won 60-42 for their first national championship.

McCracken said the Hoosiers were motivated by a telegram read over the arena's loudspeaker just before tip-off.

"The telegram, from a group of Lawrence, Kansas, businessmen, said that this would be just another game (for the Jayhawks)," said McCracken. "The boys (IU players) looked serious for a few minutes and then looked over at me and winked. Then they went to it."

IU almost didn't get a chance. The Hoosiers finished second to Purdue in the conference standings. Because there were no automatic bids, teams were selected by a committee. That committee, consisting of Butler's Tony Hinkle, Marquette's Bill Chandler, Notre Dame's George Keogan and Northwestern's K.L. Wilson, picked Indiana over the Boilermakers.

By that time, the Hoosiers had exhausted their budget, meaning there was no money left for travel (unlike now, teams paid their own way). Fortunately, athletic director Zora G. Clevenger found the funds.

Indiana finished with a 20-3 record. The Hoosiers played only three NCAA Tournament games, beating Springfield 48-24 and Duquesne 39-30 to reach the finals.

Branch McCracken (right) accepts the game ball from Kansas Coach Phog Allen after the 1940 NCAA Championship game.

"I'll never forget Kansas Coach Phog Allen after the championship game," said IU guard Bob Dro. "He came into our locker room and congratulated our team and then said his team should have won. His reasoning was that his team had control of the ball longer than we did.

"He was right about that. Kansas would come down the floor and just hold the ball. Our team was just becoming recognized as the Hurryin' Hoosiers because when one of our players was open..... he shot. That was the way McCracken wanted to play the game."

McCracken also wanted the Hoosiers focused. So, when he learned several players had snuck out of the hotel the day of the championship game to see the movie, "Gone With The Wind," he made them run laps around the hotel – an hour before tip-off.

It didn't slow them down.

Assembly Hall

IU's vision of its basketball future was inspired by a livestock pavilion in North Carolina. You read that right. The shrine of Hoosier basketball, a nationally renowned landmark, the culmination of two decades of planning, was based, in part, on a facility that housed farm animals.

But we are jumping ahead of ourselves.

Assembly Hall was to be the crown jewel of an athletic complex that would give the Hoosiers second-to-none status. Starting in the late 1940s, university officials spent almost 10 years researching a basketball facility that would be visually stunning, fan friendly, spacious and state of the art. A four-sided arena designed by one architectural firm in the early 1950s was rejected as too status-quo.

At one point, Branch McCracken wondered if planners were getting carried away.

"They are planning a Fieldhouse for us, seating around 20,000," he told the Indianapolis News in 1953. "That may be too big. I just don't know.... Maybe a 15,000 capacity Fieldhouse would be big enough."

In a 1972 football game program story, Paul "Pooch" Harrell, athletic director in the 1940s and later supervisor of athletic buildings grounds, talked about what officials wanted.

"From the very beginning, we were determined to have seating on only two sides since it is difficult to sell seats in the ends."

The difficulty had to do with the view. Back then, backboards were not see-through. Fans sitting behind the baskets couldn't tell

The original architect's scale model of Assembly Hall located adjacent to the Fieldhouse where games were played in the 1960s.

what was going on. Some schools, including IU, installed lights atop the backboards that would flash when a basket was scored, much in the manner of hockey today.

Hoosier officials figured they'd eliminate this problem, and the overall poor view behind the baskets, by putting most of the seats between the baskets.

This design, never tried before, guaranteed towering sides that would elevate fans to unsurpassed heights and, it would turn out, unexpected consequences. Harrell found the North Carolina live-stock pavilion that seemed to meet IU's needs. He passed that along to a second architectural firm and, in 1955, received a new set of plans: an "egg-shaped format" with 90 percent of the seating between the ends of the basketball floor.

It seemed perfect.

Officials liked the design so much, they also used it for Memorial Stadium. For financial reasons (football was the school's biggest money-maker and a new stadium was expected to produce more revenue), they built Memorial Stadium first. The 52,354-seat facility was completed in 1960.

In 1967, construction began on Assembly Hall on a 160-acre tract next to the Fieldhouse near the intersection of 17th Street and Fee Lane. The cost would come to almost $14 million, including $1 million for a state-of-the-art lighting system.

The 1971 basketball media guide described the arena this way:

"The new structure will be the last word in playing and spectator

Construction nears completion on Assembly Hall just a few hundred feet from the relatively new Memorial Stadium.

The finished product – the new Indiana University Assembly Hall.

facilities. It will seat approximately 17,500 spectators, all but 1,600 of them on the sides of the court, in air-conditioned, theater-type seating comfort. An overhead grid of lighting will be supplemented by side-lighting for ideal television coverage.

"A unique feature of the building is a concrete roof suspended by cables. It is composed of 4,500 concrete slabs, six feet long, three inches thick and 30 inches wide. Each weighs 600 pounds, making a roof which totals more than 2.7 million pounds.

"If you could put the entire building on scales, it would weigh in the neighborhood of 127 million pounds. It sets on limestone bedrock and required the excavation of 60,500 cubic yards of earth and 12,000 yards of rock.

"The building holds more than 30,000 yards of concrete, six million pounds of reinforcing steel and some 1,442,000 pounds of structural steel."

Columnist Corky Lamm of the Indianapolis News in Sept. 21, 1971 called Assembly Hall "the plushest basketball structure man has yet devised, a mammoth, 127-million pound conglomerate of steel and concrete that rises majestically just a push shot or two east of the 11-year-old football stadium."

Officials expected Assembly Hall to boost basketball interest.

"We've never promoted basketball before because we lacked seating, and who wants to buy a bad seat or one in the end zone," said Athletic Director Bill Orwig. "Now, we are going to start promoting because we have desirable seats for Hoosier basketball fans."

They also had desirable teams to watch. The arena's completion came with the arrival of Coach Bob Knight, who brought defensive intensity – and plenty of success – to the Hurryin' Hoosiers. The first game was Dec. 1, 1972 against Ball State. The arena was dedicated on Dec. 18 against Notre Dame. IU won both games, starting a string of victories that had, by 1995, produced a 297-37 home record. That included a school record 50-game winning streak that was snapped in 1995 by Michigan.

One of the first games in Assembly Hall. Championship banners, new goals and a new floor would all be added later.

Since opening Assembly Hall, the Hoosiers have ranked in the top 10 in national attendance every year, peaking at No. 1 in 1976 with an average of 16,892.

While Assembly Hall achieved many of the planners' goals (it remains one of college basketball's most recognized, intimidating arenas), it wasn't quite the fan-friendly facility they'd expected. The towering sides produced poor upper-level viewing and near-cardiac arrest for fans climbing the steep steps. The 17,500 seats, while plenty for the early 1970s, aren't enough for today's needs. Athletic director Clarence Doninger has talked about building a new arena, but that remains a long-term goal.

"Going into the 21st Century, Indiana needs an arena that seats over 20,000," Doninger said. "Whether that means doing something with Assembly Hall or building a new facility is something to look at."

By the Numbers

The statistics, lists and records that appear in this chapter are taken from the Indiana basketball media guide, which is produced by the Indiana Sports Information Office. The text was updated through the 1994-1995 season.

POINTS

Game – 56, Jimmy Rayl vs. Mich. St., 1962; 56, Jimmy Rayl vs. Minn., 1962 (OT)
Season – 785, Calbert Cheaney, 1993
Career – 2,613, Calbert Cheaney, 1990-93

POINTS, GAME

1. 56, Jimmy Rayl vs. Michigan State, 1963
   56, Jimmy Rayl vs. Minnesota, 1962 (OT)
3. 48, Mike Woodson vs. Illinois, 1979
4. 47, Don Schlundt vs. Ohio State, 1954
   47, Don Schlundt vs. Ohio State, 1955
   47, Steve Downing vs. Kentucky, 1972 (OT)

POINTS, SEASON

1. 785, Calbert Cheaney, 1993
2. 752, Scott May, 1976
3. 749, Steve Alford, 1987
4. 734, Calbert Cheaney, 1991
5. 729, Alan Henderson, 1995
6. 719, George McGinnis, 1971
7. 714, Jimmy Rayl, 1962
   714, Mike Woodson, 1979
9. 680, Jay Edwards, 1989
10. 661, Don Schlundt, 1953

SEASON SCORING AVERAGE

1. 29.9, George McGinnis, 1971
2. 29.8, Jimmy Rayl, 1962
3. 26.0, Don Schlundt, 1955
4. 25.5, Archie Dees, 1958
5. 25.4, Don Schlundt, 1953
6. 25.3, Jimmy Rayl, 1963
7. 25.0, Archie Dees, 1957
8. 24.3, Don Schlundt, 1954
9. 23.5, Alan Henderson, 1995
   23.5, Scott May, 1976

POINTS, CAREER

1. 2,613, Calbert Cheaney, 1990-93
2. 2,438, Steve Alford, 1984-87
3. 2,192, Don Schlundt, 1952-55
4. 2,061, Mike Woodson, 1977-80
5. 1,979, Alan Henderson, 1992-95
6. 1,741, Damon Bailey, 1991-94
7. 1,740, Kent Benson, 1974-77
8. 1,715, Eric Anderson, 1989-92
9. 1,593, Scott May, 1974-76
10. 1,590, Greg Graham, 1990-93
11. 1,549, Randy Wittman, 1979-83
12. 1,546, Archie Dees, 1956-58
13. 1,441, Walt Bellamy, 1959-61
14. 1,427, Ray Tolbert, 1978-81
15. 1,401, Jimmy Rayl, 1961-63
16. 1,357, Uwe Blab, 1982-85
17. 1,336, Ted Kitchel, 1979-83
18. 1,299, Tom Bolyard, 1961-63
19. 1,272, Joby Wright, 1969-72
20. 1,265, Steve Green, 1973-75
21. 1,252, Tom Van Arsdale, 1963-65
22. 1,240, Dick Van Arsdale, 1963-65
23. 1,220, Steve Downing, 1971-73
24. 1,195, Quinn Buckner, 1973-76

CAREER SCORING AVERAGE

1. 23.3, Don Schlundt, 1952-55
2. 22.7, Archie Dees, 1956-58
3. 20.6, Walt Bellamy, 1959-61
   20.6, Jimmy Rayl, 1961-63
5. 19.8, Mike Woodson, 1977-80
   19.8, Calbert Cheaney, 1990-93
7. 19.5, Steve Alford, 1984-87
8. 18.3, Joe Cooke, 1968-70
9. 18.2, Jay Edwards, 1988-89
10. 18.0, Tom Bolyard, 1961-63

FIELD GOALS

Game – 23, Jimmy Rayl vs. Mich. St., 1963
Season – 308, Scott May, 1976
Career – 1,018, Calbert Cheaney, 1990-93

FIELD GOALS, GAME

1. 23, Jimmy Rayl vs. Michigan State, 1963
2. 20, Jimmy Rayl vs. Minnesota, 1962 (OT)
3. 19, George McGinnis vs. No. Illinois, 1971
   19, Steve Downing vs. Kentucky, 1972 (OT)
5. 18, George McGinnis vs. Butler, 1971
   18, Steve Downing vs. Illinois, 1973
   18, Mike Woodson vs. Illinois, 1979

FIELD GOALS, SEASON

1. 308, Scott May, 1976
2. 303, Calbert Cheaney, 1993
3. 289, Calbert Cheaney, 1991
4. 284, Alan Henderson, 1995
5. 283, George McGinnis, 1971
6. 265, Mike Woodson, 1979
7. 254, Jimmy Rayl, 1962
   254, Steve Alford, 1986
9. 246, Steve Downing, 1973
10. 242, Mike Woodson, 1978

FIELD GOALS, CAREER

1. 1,018, Calbert Cheaney, 1990-93
2. 898, Steve Alford, 1984-87
3. 821, Mike Woodson, 1977-80
4. 763, Alan Henderson, 1992-95
5. 722, Kent Benson, 1974-77
6. 683, Don Schlundt, 1952-55
7. 666, Scott May, 1974-76
8. 649, Randy Wittman, 1979, 1981-83
9. 635, Eric Anderson, 1989-92
10. 593, Ray Tolbert, 1978-81

FIELD GOAL ATTEMPTS

Game – 48, Jimmy Rayl vs. Mich. St., 1963
Season – 615, George McGinnis, 1971
Career – 1,820, Calbert Cheaney, 1990-93

FIELD GOAL ATTEMPTS, GAME

1. 48, Jimmy Rayl vs. Michigan State, 1963
2. 39, Jimmy Rayl vs. Minnesota, 1962
3. 36, George McGinnis vs. Butler, 1971
4. 35, Bob Leonard vs. Iowa, 1953
   35, George McGinnis vs. No. Illinois, 1971
   35, Steve Downing vs. Kentucky, '72 (OT)

FIELD GOAL ATTEMPTS, SEASON

1. 615, George McGinnis, 1971
2. 584, Scott May, 1976
3. 580, Jimmy Rayl, 1962
4. 552, Calbert Cheaney, 1993
5. 532, Mike Woodson, 1979
6. 516, Jimmy Rayl, 1963
7. 511, Joe Cooke, 1969
8. 508, Steve Alford, 1987
9. 503, Bob Leonard, 1953
10. 485, Calbert Cheaney, 1991

FIELD GOAL ATTEMPTS, CAREER

1. 1,820, Calbert Cheaney, 1990-93
2. 1,685, Steve Alford, 1984-87
3. 1,626, Mike Woodson, 1977-80
4. 1,497, Don Schlundt, 1952-55
5. 1,413, Alan Henderson, 1992-95
6. 1,346, Kent Benson, 1974-77
7. 1,304, Bob Leonard, 1952-54
8. 1,297, Scott May, 1974-76
9. 1,252, Archie Dees, 1956-58
10. 1,238, Randy Wittman, 1979, 1981-83

FIELD GOAL PERCENTAGE

Game – 1.000, 8-8 three times, 7-7 six times
Season – .628, Matt Nover, 1993 (147-234)
Career – .571, Matt Nover, 1990-93 (370-648)

FIELD GOAL PERCENTAGE, GAME

1. 1.000 (8-8), Mike Giomi vs. N'western, 1985
   1.000 (8-8), Ricky Calloway vs. Minn., 1987
   1.000 (8-8), Matt Nover vs. W. Michigan, 1993
   1.000 (7-7), Tom Abernethy vs. S. Car., 1974
   1.000 (7-7), Stew Robinson vs. Wis., 1984
   1.000 (7-7), Chuck Franz vs. Illinois, 1984
   1.000 (7-7), Uwe Blab vs. Minnesota, 1984
   1.000 (7-7), Mike Giomi vs. Miami (O.), 1985
   1.000 (7-7), Chris Reynolds vs. Austin Peay, 1993

FIELD GOAL PERCENTAGE, SEASON

1. .628 (147-234), Matt Nover, 1993
2. .597 (284-476), Alan Henderson, 1995
3. .596 (289-485), Calbert Cheaney, 1991
4. .592 (171-289), Steve Alford, 1984
5. .588 (177-301), Ray Tolbert, 1981
6. .582 (203-349), Steve Green, 1975
7. .579 (158-273), Wayne Radford, 1978
8. .578 (237-410), Kent Benson, 1976
9. .572 (199-348), Calbert Cheaney, 1990
10. .565 (212-375), Uwe Blab, 1985

FIELD GOAL PERCENTAGE, CAREER

1. .571 (370-648), Matt Nover, 1990-93
2. .559 (1018-1820), Calbert Cheaney, 1990-93
3. .553 (331-599), Wayne Radford, 1982-85
4. .541 (545-1003), Daryl Thomas, 1984-87
5. .540 (763-1413), Alan Henderson, 1992-95
6. .538 (525-976), Steve Green, 1973-75
   .538 (347-645), Dean Garrett, 1987-88
   .538 (276-513), Joe Hillman, 1985-89
9. .536 (722-1346), Kent Benson, 1974-77
10. .533 (264-495), Tom Abernethy, 1973-76
    .533 (898-1685), Steve Alford, 1984-87

THREE-POINT FIELD GOALS

Game – 8, Steve Alford vs. Princeton, 1987; 8, Jay Edwards vs. Minnesota, 1988
Season – 107, Steve Alford, 1987
Career – 166, Damon Bailey, 1991-94

THREE-POINT FIELD GOALS, GAME

1. 8, Steve Alford vs. Princeton, 1987
   8, Jay Edwards vs. Minnesota, 1988
3. 7, Steve Alford vs. Wisconsin, 1987
   7, Steve Alford vs. Auburn, 1987
   7, Steve Alford vs. Syracuse, 1987

THREE-POINT FIELD GOALS, SEASON

1. 107, Steve Alford, 1987
2. 81, Jay Edwards, 1989
3. 59, Jay Edwards, 1988
4. 58, Brian Evans, 1995
5. 57, Greg Graham, 1993
6. 48, Damon Bailey, 1992
7. 47, Calbert Cheaney, 1993
   47, Damon Bailey, 1994

THREE-POINT FIELD GOALS, CAREER

1. 166, Damon Bailey, 1991-94
2. 148, Calbert Cheaney, 1990-93
3. 140, Jay Edwards, 1988-89
4. 124, Brian Evans, 1993-present
5. 108, Greg Graham, 1990-93
6. 107, Steve Alford, 1987

CONSECUTIVE GAMES WITH A 3-POINT FIELD GOAL

1. 20, Jay Edwards, 1989
2. 17, Steve Alford, 1987
   17, Jay Edwards, 1988
4. 16, Steve Alford, 1987
   16, Greg Graham, 1993
6. 15, Calbert Cheaney, 1991

THREE-POINT FIELD GOALS ATTEMPTS

Game – 11, five times by two different players
Season – 202, Steve Alford, 1987
Career – 380, Damon Bailey, 1991-94

THREE-POINT FIELD GOALS ATTEMPTS, GAME

1. 11, Steve Alford vs. Princeton, 1987
   11, Steve Alford vs. Wisconsin, 1987
   11, Steve Alford vs. Auburn, 1987
   11, Jay Edwards vs. Stanford, 1989
   11, Jay Edwards vs. Northwestern, 1989

THREE-POINT FIELD GOALS ATTEMPTS, SEASON

1. 202, Steve Alford, 1987
2. 181, Jay Edwards, 1989
3. 139, Brian Evans, 1995
4. 111, Greg Graham, 1993
   111, Damon Bailey, 1994
6. 110, Jay Edwards, 1988
   110, Calbert Cheaney, 1993
8. 102, Damon Bailey, 1992

THREE-POINT FIELD GOALS ATTEMPTS, CAREER

1. 380, Damon Bailey, 1991-94
2. 338, Calbert Cheaney, 1990-93
3. 298, Brian Evans, 1993-present
4. 291, Jay Edwards, 1988-89
5. 246, Greg Graham, 1990-93
6. 202, Steve Alford, 1987

THREE-POINT FIELD GOAL PERCENTAGE

Game – 1.000, Keith Smart vs. Ohio State, 1987 (5-5)
Season – .569, Pat Graham, 1994 (41-72)
Career – .530, Steve Alford, 1987 (107-202)

THREE-POINT FIELD GOAL PERCENTAGE, GAME

1. 1.000 (5-5), Keith Smart vs. Ohio State, 1987
2. .889 (8-9), Jay Edwards vs. Minnesota, '88
3. .875 (7-8), Steve Alford vs. Wisconsin, '87
4. .857 (6-7), Damon Bailey vs. Iowa, 1992
   .857 (6-7), Brian Evans at Illinois, 1994
   .857 (6-7), Pat Graham vs. Ohio State, 1994
7. .833 (5-6), Jay Edwards vs. Illinois, 1988
   .833 (5-6), Jay Edwards vs. Mich. St., 1988
   .833 (5-6), Calbert Cheaney vs. Kentucky, 1993

THREE-POINT FIELD GOAL PERCENTAGE, SEASON

1. .569 (41-72), Pat Graham, 1994
2. .536 (59-110), Jay Edwards, 1988
3. .530 (107-202), Steve Alford, 1987
4. .514 (57-111), Greg Graham, 1993
5. .490 (25-51), Calbert Cheaney, 1990
6. .473 (43-91), Calbert Cheaney, 1991
7. .471 (48-102), Damon Bailey, 1992

THREE-POINT FIELD GOAL PERCENTAGE, CAREER

1. .530 (107-202), Steve Alford, 1987
2. .481 (140-291), Jay Edwards, 1988-89
3. .480 (86-179), Pat Graham, 1990-94
4. .439 (108-246), Greg Graham, 1990-93
5. .438 (119-269), Calbert Cheaney, 1990-93
6. .437 (166-380), Damon Bailey, 1991-94

FREE THROWS

Game – 26, Greg Graham vs. Purdue, 1993
Season – 249, Don Schlundt, 1953
Career – 826, Don Schlundt, 1952-55

FREE THROWS, GAME

1. 26, Greg Graham vs. Purdue, 1993
2. 25, Don Schlundt vs. Ohio State, 1955
3. 18, Wally Choice vs. Notre Dame, 1956
   18, Ted Kitchel vs. Illinois, 1981
5. 17, Archie Dees vs. LaSalle, 1957
   17, Don Schlundt vs. Michigan, 1953
   17, Dick Van Arsdale vs. Ohio State, 1964
   17, Wayne Radford vs. Illinois, 1978
   17, Isiah Thomas vs. Michigan, 1981

CONSECUTIVE FREE THROWS, GAME

1. 18, Ted Kitchel vs. Illinois, 1981
   18, Todd Jadlow vs. Iowa, 1989
3. 16, Don Schlundt vs. Michigan State, 1955
4. 15, Don Schlundt vs. Kansas State, 1955
   15, Don Schlundt vs. Ohio State, 1954
   15, Wally Choice vs. Notre Dame, 1956
   15, Jimmy Rayl vs. Michigan, 1962

FREE THROWS, SEASON

1. 249, Don Schlundt, 1953
2. 234, Don Schlundt, 1955
3. 229, Don Schlundt, 1954
4. 206, Jimmy Rayl, 1962
5. 184, Mike Woodson, 1979

FREE THROWS, CAREER

1. 826, Don Schlundt, 1952-55
2. 535, Steve Alford, 1984-87
3. 468, Greg Graham, 1990-93
4. 447, Alan Henderson, 1992-95
5. 432, Archie Dees, 1956-58
6. 429, Calbert Cheaney, 1990-93
7. 427, Damon Bailey, 1991-94
8. 424, Eric Anderson, 1989-92
9. 419, Mike Woodson, 1977-80
10. 402, Dick Van Arsdale, 1963-65

CONSECUTIVE FREE THROWS

1. 38, Pat Graham, 1990-91
2. 37, Keith Smart, 1988
3. 32, Jimmy Rayl, 1962
   32, John Ritter, 1971-72
5. 31, Steve Alford, 1984-85

FREE THROW ATTEMPTS

Game – 30, Don Schlundt vs. Ohio State, 1955
Season – 310, Don Schlundt, 1953
Career – 1,076, Don Schlundt, 1952-55

FREE THROW ATTEMPTS, GAME

1. 30, Don Schlundt vs. Ohio State, 1955
2. 28, Greg Graham vs. Purdue, 1993
3. 23, Wally Choice vs. Notre Dame, 1956
4. 21, Archie Dees vs. LaSalle, 1957
   21, Jimmy Rayl vs. Northwestern, 1962
   21, Isiah Thomas vs. Michigan, 1981

FREE THROW ATTEMPTS, SEASON

1. 310, Don Schlundt, 1953
2. 299, Don Schlundt, 1955
3. 296, Don Schlundt, 1954
4. 251, Alan Henderson, 1995
5. 249, George McGinnis, 1971

FREE THROW ATTEMPTS, CAREER

1. 1,076, Don Schlundt, 1952-55
2. 692, Alan Henderson, 1992-95
3. 611, Greg Graham, 1990-93
4. 596, Steve Alford, 1984-87
5. 578, Eric Anderson, 1989-92
6. 566, Damon Bailey, 1991-94
7. 543, Calbert Cheaney, 1990-93
8. 537, Mike Woodson, 1977-80
9. 522, Archie Dees, 1956-58
10. 507, Dick Van Arsdale, 1963-65

FREE THROW PERCENTAGE

Game – 1.000, 31 times 10-10 or better
Season – .921, Steve Alford, 1985 (116-126)
Career – .898, Steve Alford, 1984-87 (535-596)

FREE THROW PERCENTAGE, GAME

1. 1.000 - 31 times 10 of 10 or better
   18-18, Ted Kitchel vs. Illinois, 1981
   15-15, Don Schlundt vs. Kansas, 1955
   15-15, Jimmy Rayl vs. Michigan, 1962
   14-14, Don Schlundt vs. Minnesota, 1954
   14-14, Damon Bailey vs. Ohio State, 1992

FREE THROW PERCENTAGE, SEASON

1. .921 (116-126), Steve Alford, 1985
2. .913 (137-150), Steve Alford, 1984
3. .908 (69-76), Jay Edwards, 1988
4. .900 (63-70), Jon McGlocklin, 1965
5. .893 (100-112), Pat Graham, 1994
6. .889 (48-54), Sam Gee, 1958
   .889 (160-180), Steve Alford, 1987
8. .883 (68-77), Rick Ford, 1970
9. .874 (160-183), Ted Kitchel, 1982

FREE THROW PERCENTAGE, CAREER

1. .898 (535-596), Steve Alford, 1984-87
2. .862 (257-298), John Ritter, 1971-73
3. .857 (359-419), Ted Kitchel, 1980-83
4. .856 (154-180), Keith Smart, 1987-88
5. .855 (276-323), Pat Graham, 1990-94
6. .846 (99-117), Todd Leary, 1990-94
7. .845 (232-274), Jay Edwards, 1988-89
8. .835 (395-473), Jimmy Rayl, 1961-63
9. .828 (432-522), Archie Dees, 19956-58
10. .820 (128-156), Rick Ford, 1969-72

REBOUNDS

Game – 33, Walt Bellamy vs. Michigan, 1961
Season – 428, Walt Bellamy, 1961
Career – 1,091, Alan Henderson, 1992-95

REBOUNDS, GAME

1. 33, Walt Bellamy vs. Michigan, 1961
2. 28, Walt Bellamy vs. Wisconsin, 1961
3. 26, Dick Neal vs. Wisconsin, 1957
   26, Dick Van Arsdale vs. Missouri, 1964
   26, Steve Downing vs. Ball State, 1972

REBOUNDS, SEASON

1. 428, Walt Bellamy, 1961
2. 377, Steve Downing, 1972
3. 352, George McGinnis, 1971
4. 345, Archie Dees, 1958
5. 335, Walt Bellamy, 1959
6. 325, Walt Bellamy, 1960
7. 317, Archie Dees, 1957
8. 308, Alan Henderson, 1994

REBOUNDS, SEASON AVERAGE

1. 17.8, Walt Bellamy, 1961
2. 15.2, Walt Bellamy, 1959
3. 15.1, Steve Downing, 1972
4. 14.7, George McGinnis, 1971
5. 14.4, Archie Dees, 1958
   14.4, Archie Dees, 1957
7. 13.5, Walt Bellamy, 1960
8. 12.4, Dick Van Arsdale, 1964
9. 12.3, Tom Van Arsdale, 1964
10. 10.6, Steve Downing, 1973

REBOUNDS, CAREER

1. 1,091, Alan Henderson, 1992-95
2. 1,088, Walt Bellamy, 1959-61
3. 1,031, Kent Benson, 1974-77
4. 914, Archie Dees, 19956-58
5. 889, Steve Downing, 1971-73
6. 874, Ray Tolbert, 1978-81
7. 860, Don Schlundt, 1952-55
8. 826, Eric Anderson, 1989-92

ASSISTS

Game – 15, Keith Smart vs. Auburn, 1987
Season – 197, Isiah Thomas, 1981
Career – 542, Quinn Buckner, 1973-76

ASSISTS, GAME

1. 15, Keith Smart vs. Auburn, 1987
2. 14, Quinn Buckner vs. Illinois, 1974
   14, Bobby Wilkerson vs. Michigan, 1976
   14, Isiah Thomas vs. Maryland, 1981
   14, Stew Robinson vs. Marquette, 1985

ASSISTS, SEASON

1. 197, Isiah Thomas, 1981
2. 177, Quinn Buckner, 1975
3. 171, Bobby Wilkerson, 1976
4. 168, Jamal Meeks, 1991
5. 159, Isiah Thomas, 1980

ASSISTS, SEASON AVERAGE

1. 5.6, Isiah Thomas, 1981
2. 5.5, Quinn Buckner, 1975
   5.5, Isiah Thomas, 1980
4. 5.4, Quinn Buckner, 1974
5. 5.3, Bobby Wilkerson, 1976

ASSISTS, CAREER

1. 542, Quinn Buckner, 1973-76
2. 474, Jamal Meeks, 1989-92
   474, Damon Bailey, 1991-94
4. 432, Randy Wittman, 1979, 1981-83
5. 391, Stew Robinson, 1983-86
6. 385, Steve Alford, 1984-87
7. 356, Isiah Thomas, 1980-81
   356, Chris Reynolds, 1990-93
9. 336, Butch Carter, 1977-80
10. 325, Jim Wisman, 1975-78

STEALS

Game – 9, Scott May vs. Michigan, 1976
Season – 74, Isiah Thomas, 1981
Career – 178, Steve Alford, 1984-87

STEALS, GAME

1. 9, Scott May vs. Michigan, 1976
2. 8, Steve Alford vs. Butler, 1985
3. 7, Jim Crews vs. UCLA, 1976

STEALS, SEASON

1. 74, Isiah Thomas, 1981
2. 65, Quinn Buckner, 1976
3. 62, Isiah Thomas, 1980
4. 53, Mike Woodson, 1979
5. 50, Steve Alford, 1986

STEALS, SEASON AVERAGE

1. 2.2, Isiah Thomas, 1981
2. 2.1, Isiah Thomas, 1980
3. 2.0, Quinn Buckner, 1976

STEALS, CAREER

1. 178, Steve Alford, 1984-87
2. 151, Greg Graham, 1990-93
3. 148, Alan Henderson, 1992-95
4. 142, Mike Woodson, 1977-80
5. 136, Isiah Thomas, 1980-81
6. 135, Chris Reynolds, 1990-93
7. 132, Damon Bailey, 1991-94
8. 120, Randy Wittman, 1979, 1981-83
9. 117, Calbert Cheaney, 1990-93
10. 106, Jim Thomas, 1980-83

BLOCKS

Game – 8, Dean Garrett vs. Montana State, 1987; 8,
Dean Garrett vs. Iowa, 1988
Season – 99, Dean Garrett, 1988
Career – 213, Alan Henderson, 1992-95

BLOCKS, GAME

1. 8, Dean Garrett vs. Montana State, 1987
   8, Dean Garrett vs. Iowa, 1988
3. 7, Uwe Blab vs. Tennessee Tech, 1984
   7, Uwe Blab vs. Ball State, 1984
   7, Dean Garrett vs. UNC-Wilmington, '87
   7, Dean Garrett vs. James Madison, 1988
   7, Dean Garrett vs. E. Kentucky, 1988

BLOCKS, SEASON

1. 99, Dean Garrett, 1988
2. 93, Dean Garrett, 1987
3. 72, Uwe Blab, 1985
4. 69, Uwe Blab, 1984
5. 64, Alan Henderson, 1995
6. 56, Alan Henderson, 1994
7. 51, Eric Anderson, 1991

BLOCKS, SEASON AVERAGE

1. 3.4, Dean Garrett, 1988
2. 2.7, Dean Garrett, 1987
3. 2.2, Uwe Blab, 1985
   2.2, Uwe Blab, 1984

BLOCKS, CAREER

1. 213, Alan Henderson, 1992-95
2. 204, Uwe Blab, 1982-85
3. 192, Dean Garrett, 1987-88
4. 155, Ray Tolbert, 1978-81
5. 134, Eric Anderson, 1989-92

POINTS

Game – 122, at Ohio State, 1959, 122, vs. Notre
    Dame, 1962
Season – 3,028, 1993

POINTS, GAME

1. 122 at Ohio State, 1959
   122 vs. Notre Dame, 1962
3. 118 vs. Iowa, 1990
4. 117 vs. Tennessee Tech, 1994
5. 116 vs. Iowa, 1988
6. 115 vs. Iowa State, 1990
7. 114 vs. Wisconsin, 1976
8. 113 vs. Purdue, 1953
   113 vs. Michigan State, 1963
   113 vs. Tennessee Tech, 1975
   113 vs. No. Illinois, 1971

POINTS, SEASON

1. 3,028 in 1993   6. 2,747 in 1989
2. 2,882 in 1991   7. 2,628 in 1976
3. 2,837 in 1992   8. 2,451 in 1981
4. 2,817 in 1975   9. 2,428 in 1994
5. 2,806 in 1987   10. 2,349 in 1985

POINTS, SEASON AVERAGE

1. 91.7 in 1965   6. 84.8 in 1991
2. 90.8 in 1971   7. 84.7 in 1963
3. 88.0 in 1975   8. 83.4 in 1992
4. 87.0 in 1962   9. 81.7 in 1967
5. 86.5 in 1993   10. 82.5 in 1987

FIELD GOALS

Game – 52, vs. South Dakota, 1977
Season – 1,148, 1975

FIELD GOALS, GAME

1. 52 vs. South Dakota, 1977
2. 51 vs. Notre Dame, 1962
   51 vs. Butler, 1971
4. 50 vs. Ohio State, 1959
   50 vs. Michigan State, 1975
6. 49 vs. Michigan State, 1965
7. 48 vs. Michigan State, 1963
   48 vs. No. Illinois, 1971
9. 47 vs. Illinois, 1975
   47 vs. Wisconsin, 1976

FIELD GOALS, SEASON

1. 1,148 in 1975   6. 990 in 1992
2. 1,083 in 1976   7. 978 in 1981
3. 1,076 in 1993   8. 956 in 1985
4. 1,043 in 1991   9. 954 in 1989
5. 1,033 in 1987   10. 921 in 1974

FIELD GOAL ATTEMPTS

Game – 52, vs. South Dakota, 1977
Season – 1,148, 1975

FIELD GOAL ATTEMPTS, GAME

1. 124 vs. Texas Christian, 1951
2. 114 vs. Purdue, 1953
3. 110 vs. Iowa, 1950
   110 vs. Michigan State, 1964
5. 107 vs. Iowa, 1949
   107 vs. Northwestern, 1951

FIELD GOAL ATTEMPTS, SEASON

1. 2,256 in 1975   6. 1,975 in 1967
2. 2,094 in 1976   7. 1,974 in 1992
3. 2,062 in 1993   8. 1,955 in 1991
4. 2,019 in 1953   9. 1,947 in 1969
5. 2,015 in 1987   10. 1,939 in 1961

FIELD GOAL PERCENTAGE

Game – .712, vs. Michigan State, 1988
Season – .537, 1986

FIELD GOAL PERCENTAGE, GAME

1. .712 (42-59) vs. Michigan State, 1988
2. .711 (32-45) vs. Texas Tech, 1979
3. .711 (27-38) vs. Michigan State, 1989
4. .697 (23-33) vs. Illinois, 1983
5. .695 (32-46) vs. Ohio State, 1983
6. .686 (35-51) vs. St. Joseph's, 1981
7. .678 (40-59) vs. Illinois, 1991
8. .667 (52-78) vs. South Dakota, 1977
   .667 (38-57) vs. Wisconsin, 1981
   .667 (18-27) vs. Iowa, 1984
   .667 (36-54) vs. Michigan, 1985
   .667 (32-48) vs. Michigan, 1986

FIELD GOAL PERCENTAGE, SEASON

1. .537 in 1986   8. .517 in 1976
2. .534 in 1991   9. .515 in 1988
3. .530 in 1981   10. .514 in 1990
4. .528 in 1985
5. .522 in 1983
   .522 in 1984
   .522 in 1993

THREE-POINT FIELD GOALS

Game – 11, vs. Wisconsin, 1987
Season – 197, 1993

THREE-POINT FIELD GOALS, GAME

1. 11, vs. Wisconsin, 1987
2. 10, vs. Princeton, 1987
   10, vs. Iowa, 1993
   10, vs. Penn State, 1993
   10, vs. Michigan State, 1993
   10, vs. Tennessee Tech, 1994
   10, vs. Illinois, 1994
   10, vs. Iowa, 1994
   10, vs. Temple, 1994
   10, vs. Iowa, 1995

THREE-POINT FIELD GOALS, SEASON

1. 197 in 1993   6. 120 in 1991
2. 182 in 1994   7. 107 in 1995
3. 162 in 1992   8. 93 in 1990
4. 130 in 1987   9. 84 in 1988
5. 121 in 1989

THREE-POINT FIELD GOAL ATTEMPTS

Game – 24, vs. Penn State, 1993
Season – 464, 1993

THREE-POINT FIELD GOAL ATTEMPTS, GAME

1. 24, vs. Penn State, 1993
2. 23, vs. Iowa, 1993
3. 20, vs. Temple, 1994
4. 19, vs. Boston University, 1992
   19, vs. Indiana State, 1992
   19, vs. Northwestern, 1993
   19, vs. Michigan State, 1993
   19, vs. Iowa, 1994
   19, vs. Ohio State, 1994
10. 18, vs. Florida State, 1992
    18, vs. Penn State, 1993

THREE-POINT FIELD GOAL ATTEMPTS, SEASON

1. 464 in 1993
2. 401 in 1994
3. 384 in 1992
4. 297 in 1995
5. 294 in 1991
6. 256 in 1987
   256 in 1989
8. 213 in 1990

THREE-POINT FIELD GOAL PERCENTAGE

Game – .889, vs. Minnesota, 1988
Season – .508, 1987

THREE-POINT FIELD GOAL PERCENTAGE, GAME

1. .889 (8-9), vs. Minnesota, 1988
2. .833 (10-12), vs. Tennessee Tech, 1994
   .833 (5-6), vs. Vanderbilt, 1987
   .833 (5-6), vs. Notre Dame, 1988
   .833 (5-6), vs. Illinois, 1988
   .833 (5-6), vs. Michigan State, 1988
   .833 (5-6), vs. Michigan State, 1989
   .833 (5-6), vs. George Mason, 1989
   .833 (5-6), vs. Michigan State, 1991
10. .800 (8-10), vs. Ohio State, 1987

THREE-POINT FIELD GOAL PERCENTAGE, SEASON

1. .508 (130-256) in 1987
2. .473 (121-256) in 1989
3. .467 (84-180) in 1988
4. .454 (182-401) in 1994
5. .437 (93-213) in 1990
6. .425 (197-464) in 1993
7. .422 (162-384) in 1992

FREE THROWS

Game – 43, vs. Michigan, 1955
Season – 718, 1989

FREE THROWS, GAME

1. 43 vs. Michigan, 1955
2. 42 vs. Purdue, 1953
   42 vs. Minnesota, 1991
4. 40 vs. Ohio State, 1955
5. 38 vs. Butler, 1953
   38 vs. Northwestern, 1952
   38 vs. Michigan State, 1952

FREE THROWS, SEASON

1. 718 in 1989
2. 695 in 1992
3. 679 in 1993
4. 676 in 1991
5. 638 in 1953
6. 610 in 1987

FREE THROW ATTEMPTS

Game – 60, vs. Michigan, 1955
Season – 978, 1989

FREE THROW ATTEMPTS, GAME

1. 60 vs. Michigan, 1955
2. 56 vs. Ohio State, 1956
3. 55 vs. Purdue, 1953
4. 53 vs. Minnesota, 1954
5. 51 vs. Minnesota, 1991

FREE THROW ATTEMPTS, SEASON

1. 978 in 1989
2. 949 in 1992
3. 947 in 1993
4. 927 in 1991
5. 910 in 1953
6. 907 in 1954

FREE THROW PERCENTAGE

Game – 1.000, vs. OSU, 1988, vs. DePaul, 1964
Season – .768, 1965

FREE THROW PERCENTAGE, GAME

1. 1.000 (18-18) vs. Ohio State, 1988
   1.000 (12-12) vs DePaul, 1964
3. .954 (21-22) vs. Minnesota, 1988
4. .952 (20-21) vs. Wisconsin, 1964
   .952 (20-21) vs. Northwestern, 1965
6. .950 (19-20) vs. Earlham, 1948
   .950 (19-20) vs. Illinois, 1991
8. .944 (17-18) vs. Toledo, 1977
   .944 (17-18) vs. Illinois, 1981
10. .941 (16-17) vs. Illinois, 1982

FREE THROW PERCENTAGE, SEASON

1. .768 in 1965
2. .767 in 1987
3. .755 in 1966
4. .750 in 1994
4. .746 in 1983
5. .744 in 1981

CONSECUTIVE FREE THROWS

1. 25 vs. Michigan, 1963

REBOUNDS

Game – 95, vs. Michigan, 1961
Season – 1,433, 1975

REBOUNDS, GAME

1. 95 vs. Michigan, 1961
2. 89 vs. Purdue, 1951
3. 75 vs. Wisconsin, 1957

REBOUNDS, SEASON

1. 1,433 in 1975
2. 1,363 in 1961
3. 1,354 in 1969
4. 1,337 in 1967
5. 1,324 in 1976
6. 1,313 in 1962
7. 1,307 in 1971
8. 1,281 in 1993
9. 1,268 in 1992

REBOUNDING AVERAGE

1. 56.8 in 1961
2. 56.4 in 1969
3. 54.7 in 1962
4. 54.5 in 1971
5. 52.0 in 1964

ASSISTS

Game – 30, vs. Northwestern, 1981
Season – 655, 1976

ASSISTS, GAME

1. 30 vs. Northwestern, 1981
2. 29 vs. St. Joseph's, 1981
   29 vs. Grambling, 1983
   29 vs. Northwestern, 1987
   29 vs. Northeastern, 1991
   29 vs. St. John's, 1993
   29 vs. Iowa, 1995
8. 28 vs. Michigan, 1982
   28 vs. Iowa, 1988

ASSISTS, SEASON

1. 655 in 1976
2. 636 in 1991
3. 620 in 1993
4. 603 in 1975
5. 592 in 1985
6. 590 in 1992
7. 582 in 1981
8. 554 in 1979
9. 543 in 1987
10. 528 in 1989

Game – 11, vs. Iowa, 1988
Season – 135, 1987

BLOCKS, GAME

1. 11 vs. Iowa, 1988
2. 10 vs. Texas A&M. 1984
   10 vs. Ball State, 1984
   10 vs. James Madison, 1988
   10 vs. Arkansas-Little Rock, 1989
6. 9 vs. Miami (OH), 1980
   9 vs. Montana State, 1987
   9 vs. Eastern Kentucky, 1994
   9 vs. Iowa, 1994
   9 vs. Northwestern, 1994

BLOCKS, SEASON

1. 146 in 1995	6. 116 in 1989
2. 135 in 1987	7. 111 in 1991
3. 131 in 1988	8. 102 in 1985
4. 125 in 1994	9. 99 in 1993
5. 122 in 1992	10. 89 in 1984

STEALS

Game – 19, vs. Northwestern, 1987
Season – 250, 1992

STEALS, GAME

1. 19 vs. Northwestern, 1987
2. 18 vs. California, 1981
   18 vs. Iowa, 1991
4. 17 vs. Indiana State, 1992
5. 16 vs. Xavier (OH), 1980
6. 15 vs. Iowa, 1978
   15 vs. Northwestern, 1986
8. 14 five times

STEALS, SEASON

1. 250 in 1992	6. 207 in 1979
2. 247 in 1991	7. 205 in 1978
3. 224 in 1981	8. 201 in 1989
4. 218 in 1993	9. 197 in 1980
5. 215 in 1987	10. 188 in 1985

VICTORIES

1. 32-0 in 1976	6. 27-8 in 1989
2. 31-1 in 1975	27-7 in 1992
31-4 in 1993	8. 26-9 in 1981
4. 30-4 in 1987	9. 24-6 in 1983
5. 29-5 in 1991	10. 23-3 in 1953
	23-5 in 1974

SCORING

Year	Player	G	Pts	Avg
1940	Paul Armstrong	23	203	8.8
1941	William Menke	20	176	8.8
1942	Ed Denton	21	173	8.2
1943	Ralph Hamilton	20	249	12.5
1944	Paul Shields	21	178	8.5
1945	Al Kralovansky	21	193	9.2
1946	John Wallace	21	302	14.4
1947	Ralph Hamilton	20	267	13.4
1948	Don Ritter	20	275	13.8
1949	Bill Garrett	22	220	10.0
1950	Bill Garrett	22	283	12.9
1951	Bill Garrett	22	289	13.1
1952	Don Schlundt	22	376	17.1
1953	Don Schlundt	26	661	25.4
1954	Don Schlundt	24	583	24.3
1955	Don Schlundt	22	572	26.0
1956	Wally Choice	22	463	21.0
1957	Archie Dees	22	550	25.0
1958	Archie Dees	24	613	25.5
1959	Walt Bellamy	22	382	17.4
1960	Walt Bellamy	24	537	22.4
1961	Walt Bellamy	24	522	21.8
1962	Jimmy Rayl	24	714	29.8
1963	Jimmy Rayl	24	608	25.3
1964	Dick VanArsdale	24	535	22.3
1965	Tom VanArsdale	24	441	18.4
1966	Max Walker	23	380	16.5
1967	Butch Joyner	26	481	18.5
1968	Vern Payne	24	354	14.8
1969	Joe Cooke	24	523	21.8
1970	Jim Harris	24	434	18.1
1971	George McGinnis	24	719	29.9
1972	Joby Wright	25	498	19.9
1973	Steve Downing	28	563	20.1
1974	Steve Green	28	467	16.7
1975	Steve Green	31	516	16 6
1976	Scott May	32	752	23 5
1977	Mike Woodson	27	500	18.5
1978	Mike Woodson	29	577	19.9
1979	Mike Woodson	34	714	21.0
1980	Isiah Thomas	29	423	14.6
1981	Isiah Thomas	34	545	16.0
1982	Ted Kitchel	29	568	19.6
1983	Randy Wittman	30	569	18.9
1984	Steve Alford	31	479	15 5
1985	Steve Alford	32	580	18.1
1986	Steve Alford	28	630	22.5
1987	Steve Alford	34	749	22.0
1988	Dean Garrett	29	467	16.1
1989	Jay Edwards	34	680	20.0
1990	Calbert Cheaney	29	495	17.1
1991	Calbert Cheaney	34	734	21.6
1992	Calbert Cheaney	34	599	17.6
1993	Calbert Cheaney	35	785	22.4
1994	Damon Bailey	30	589	19.6
1995	Alan Henderson	30	711	23.7

REBOUNDING

Year	Player	G	Rebs	Avg
1951	Bill Garrett	22	186	8.5
1952	Don Schlundt	22	158	7.2
1953	Charles Kraak	26	235	10.7
1954	Don Schlundt	24	267	11.1
1955	Don Schlundt	22	215	9.8
1956	Archie Dees	22	252	12.6
1957	Archie Dees	22	317	14.4
1958	Archie Dees	24	345	14.4
1959	Walt Bellamy	22	335	15.2
1960	Walt Bellamy	24	324	13.5
1961	Walt Bellamy	24	428	17.8
1962	Charley Hall	24	247	10.3
1963	Tom VanArsdale	24	223	9.3
1964	Dick VanArsdale	24	298	12.4
1965	Dick VanArsdale	24	208	8.7
1966	Butch Joyner	24	190	7.9
1967	Butch Joyner	26	272	10.5
1968	Bill DeHeer	24	250	10.4
1969	Ken Johnson	24	292	12.1
1970	Ken Johnson	24	252	10.5
1971	George McGinnis	24	352	14.7
1972	Steve Downing	25	377	15.1
1973	Steve Downing	28	296	10.6
1974	Kent Benson	27	222	8.2
1975	Kent Benson	32	286	8.9
1976	Kent Benson	32	282	8.8
1977	Kent Benson	23	241	10.8
1978	Ray Tolbert	29	201	6.9
1979	Ray Tolbert	34	241	7.1
1980	Ray Tolbert	29	208	7.2
1981	Ray Tolbert	35	224	6.4
1982	Jim Thomas	29	181	6.2
1983	Jim Thomas	30	159	5.3
1984	Uwe Blab	31	190	6.1
1985	Uwe Blab	33	207	6.3
1986	Andre Harris	29	162	5.6
1987	Dean Garrett	34	288	8.5
1988	Dean Garrett	29	246	8.5
1989	Eric Anderson	34	208	6.1
1990	Eric Anderson	29	202	7.0
1991	Eric Anderson	34	243	7.1
1992	Alan Henderson	33	238	7.2
1993	Alan Henderson	30	243	8.1
1994	Alan Henderson	30	308	10.3
1995	Alan Henderson	30	292	9.7

FIELD GOAL PERCENTAGE

Year	Player	G	Pct
1953	Don Schlundt	26	.432
1954	Don Schlundt	24	.500
1955	Don Schlundt	22	.448
1956	Wally Choice	22	.510
1957	Dick Neal	19	.486
1958	Archie Dees	24	.479
1959	Walt Bellamy	22	.512
1960	Walt Bellamy	24	.535
1961	Walt Bellamy	24	.501
1962	Tom Bolyard	24	.443
1963	Tom Bolyard	24	.478
1964	Jon McGlocklin	24	.460
1965	Jon McGlocklin	23	.543
1966	Gary Grieger	22	.485
1967	Erv Inniger	17	.515
1968	Bill DeHeer	24	.504
1969	Kenny Johnson	24	.445
1970	Joe Cooke	12	.480
1971	Steve Downing	23	.505
1972	John Ritter	25	.510
1973	Steve Downing	28	.520
1974	Steve Green	28	.545
1975	Steve Green	31	.582
1976	Kent Benson	32	.578
1977	Mike Woodson	27	.521
1978	Wayne Radford	29	.579
1979	Ray Tolbert	34	.544
1980	Butch Carter	29	.547
1981	Ray Tolbert	35	.588
1982	Uwe Blab	24	.556
1983	Randy Wittman	30	.543
1984	Steve Alford	31	.592
1985	Uwe Blab	33	.565
1986	Daryl Thomas	26	.561
1987	Dean Garrett	34	.542
1988	Dean Garrett	29	.535
1989	Eric Anderson	34	.545
1990	Calbert Cheaney	29	.572
1991	Calbert Cheaney	34	.596
1992	Calbert Cheaney	34	.522
1993	Matt Nover	35	.628
1994	Todd Lindeman	29	.548
1995	Alan Henderson	30	.606

THREE-POINT FIELD GOAL PERCENTAGE

Year	Player	G	Pct.
1983	Ted Kitchel	24	.656
1987	Steve Alford	34	.530
1988	Jay Edwards	23	.536
1989	Joe Hillman	34	.581
1990	Calbert Cheaney	29	.490
1991	Calbert Cheaney	34	.473
1992	Damon Bailey	34	.471
1993	Greg Graham	35	.514
1994	Pat Graham	28	.569
1995	Charlie Miller	30	.533

FREE THROW PERCENTAGE

Year	Player	G	Pct.
1953	Don Schlundt	26	.803
1954	Don Schlundt	24	.774
1955	Don Schlundt	22	.783
1956	Hallie Bryant	21	.831
1957	Archie Dees	22	.842
1958	Samuel Gee	18	.889
1959	Herbie Lee	22	.741
1960	Frank Radovich	24	.745
1961	Walt Bellamy	24	.647
1962	Jimmy Rayl	24	.834
1963	Jimmy Rayl	24	.873
1964	Dick VanArsdale	24	.803
1965	Dick VanArsdale	24	.852
1966	Gary Grieger	22	.817
1967	Jack Johnson	26	.855
1968	Earl Schneider	24	.769
1969	Joe Cooke	24	.758
1970	Rick Ford	20	.883
1971	Jim Harris	24	.763
1972	John Ritter	25	.873
1973	John Ritter	28	.873
1974	John Laskowski	28	.774
1975	Steve Green	31	.797
1976	Scott May	32	.782
1977	Mike Woodson	27	.792
1978	Wayne Radford	29	.770
1979	Mike Woodson	34	.763
1980	Isiah Thomas	29	.772
1981	Ted Kitchel	34	.854
1982	Ted Kitchel	29	.874
1983	Ted Kitchel	24	.859
1984	Steve Alford	31	.913
1985	Steve Alford	32	.921
1986	Steve Alford	28	.871
1987	Steve Alford	34	.889
1988	Jay Edwards	23	.908
1989	Jay Edwards	34	.823
1990	Greg Graham	29	.778
1991	Pat Graham	34	.850
1992	Eric Anderson	34	.807
1993	Greg Graham	35	.825
1994	Pat Graham	28	.893
1995	Brian Evans	30	.787

STEALS

Year	Player	G	Stls	Avg
1976	Quinn Buckner	32	65	2.0
1977	Mike Woodson	27	40	1.5
1978	Jim Wisman	29	40	1.4
1979	Mike Woodson	34	53	1.6
1980	IsiahThomas	29	62	2.1
1981	Isiah Thomas	34	74	2.2
1982	Jim Thomas	29	38	1.3
1983	Jim Thomas	30	35	1.2
1984	Steve Alford	31	45	1.5
1985	Steve Alford	32	44	1.4
1986	Steve Alford	28	50	1.8
1987	Daryl Thomas	34	45	1.3
1988	Keith Smart	29	27	0.9
1989	Joe Hillman	34	42	1.2
1990	Calbert Cheaney	29	24	0.8
	Chris Reynolds	28	24	0.9
1991	Damon Bailey	34	39	1.1
1992	Chris Reynolds	33	49	1.5
1993	Greg Graham	35	47	1.3
1994	Damon Bailey	30	45	1.5
1995	Alan Henderson	30	40	1.3

ASSISTS

Year	Player	G	Asst	Avg
1971	Jim Harris	24	72	3.0
1972	Bootsie White	24	104	4.3
1973	Quinn Buckner	28	82	2.9
1974	Quinn Buckner	28	150	5.4
1975	Quinn Buckner	32	177	5.5
1976	Bobby Wilkerson	32	171	5.3
1977	Jim Wisman	26	130	5.0
1978	Jim Wisman	29	115	4.0
1979	Butch Carter	33	151	4.6
1980	Isiah Thomas	29	159	5.5
1981	Isiah Thomas	34	197	5.8
1982	Jim Thomas	29	103	3.5
1983	Tony Brown	29	116	4.0
1984	Stew Robinson	30	104	3.5
1985	Stew Robinson	29	134	4.6
1986	Winston Morgan	29	133	4.6
1987	Steve Alford	34	123	3.6
1988	Joe Hillman	27	105	3.9
1989	Joe Hillman	34	132	3.9
1990	Jamal Meeks	28	106	3.8
1991	Jamal Meeks	34	168	4.9
1992	Jamal Meeks	32	133	4.2
1993	Damon Bailey	35	144	4.1
1994	Damon Bailey	30	129	4.3
1995	Brian Evans	30	100	3.3

BLOCKS

Year	Player	G	Blks	Avg
1976	Kent Benson	32	39	1.2
1977	Kent Benson	23	28	1.2
1978	Ray Tolbert	29	39	1.3
1979	Ray Tolbert	34	45	1.3
1980	Ray Tolbert	29	33	1.1
1981	Ray Tolbert	38	35	0.9
1982	Uwe Blab	24	16	0.8
	John Flowers	29	16	0.6
1983	Uwe Blab	30	39	1.3
1984	Uwe Blab	31	69	2.2
1985	Uwe Blab	33	72	2.2
1986	Andre Harris	29	48	1.7
1987	Dean Garrett	34	93	2.7
1988	Dean Garrett	29	99	3.4
1989	Eric Anderson	34	33	0.9
1990	Eric Anderson	29	15	0.5
	Calbert Cheaney	29	15	0.5
1991	Eric Anderson	34	51	1.5
1992	Alan Henderson	33	50	1.5
1993	Alan Henderson	30	43	1.4
1994	Alan Henderson	30	56	1.9
1995	Alan Henderson	30	61	2.0

ALL-AMERICANS, MVPS

ALL-AMERICANS

1993	Calbert Cheaney
1992	Calbert Cheaney
1991	Calbert Cheaney
1989	Jay Edwards
1987	Steve Alford
1986	Steve Alford
1983	Ted Kitchel
1983	Randy Wittman
1982	Ted Kitchel
1982	Landon Turner
1981	Isiah Thomas
1980	Mike Woodson
1979	Mike Woodson
1977	Kent Benson
1976	Scott May
1976	Kent Benson
1976	Quinn Buckner
1975	Scott May
1975	Kent Benson
1975	Quinn Buckner
1975	Steve Green
1974	Steve Green
1973	Steve Downing
1971	George McGinnis

1965	Dick VanArsdale
1965	Tom VanArsdale
1963	Jimmy Rayl
1962	Jimmy Rayl
1961	Walt Bellamy
1960	Walt Bellamy
1958	Archie Dees
1957	Archie Dees
1955	Don Schlundt
1954	Bob Leonard
1954	Don Schlundt
1953	Bob Leonard
1953	Don Schlundt
1951	Bill Garrett
1950	Lou Watson
1947	Ralph Hamilton
1946	John Wallace
1942	Andy Zimmer
1940	Bill Menke
1940	Marv Huffman
1938	Ernie Andres
1937	Ken Gunning
1936	Vern Huffman
1930	Branch McCracken
1929	Jim Strickland
1921	Everett Dean

BIG TEN MOST VALUABLE PLAYERS

1993	Calbert Cheaney
1987	Steve Alford
1983	Randy Wittman
1981	Ray Tolbert
1980	Mike Woodson
1977	Kent Benson
1976	Scott May
1975	Scott May
1973	Steve Downing
1958	Archie Dees
1957	Archie Dees
1953	Don Schlundt

YEAR BY YEAR RECORDS

Season	Coach	Record
1900-01	J.H. Horne	1-4
1901-02	Phelps Darby	4-4
1902-03	Willis Coval	8-4
1903-04	Willis Coval	5-4
1904-05	Z.G. Clevenger	5-12, Big Ten 1-1
1905-06	Z.G. Clevenger	7-9, Big Ten 2-2
1906-07	James Sheldon	9-5, Big Ten 0-0
1907-08	Ed Cook	9-6, Big Ten 2-4
1908-09	Robert Harris	5-9, Big Ten 2-6
1909-10	John Georgen	5-8, Big Ten 3-7
1910-11	Oscar Rackle	11-5, Big Ten 5-5
1911-12	James Kase	6-11, Big Ten 1-9
1912-13	Arthur Powell	5-11, Big Ten 0-10
1913-14	Arthur Berndt	2-12, Big Ten 1-11
1914-15	Arthur Berndt	4-9, Big Ten 1-9
1915-16	Allen Willisford	6-7, Big Ten 3-5
1916-17	G.S. Lowman	13-6, Big Ten 3-5
1917-18	Dana M. Evans	10-4, Big Ten 3-3
1918-19	Dana M. Evans	10-7, Big Ten 4-6
1919-20	Eward O. Stiehm	13-8, Big Ten 6-4
1920-21	George W. Lewis	15-6, Big Ten 6-5
1921-22	George W. Lewis	10-10, Big Ten 3-7
1922-23	Leslie Mann	8-7, Big Ten 5-7
1923-24	Leslie Mann	11-6, Big Ten 7-5
1924-25	Everett Dean	12-5, Big Ten 8-4
1925-26	Everett Dean	12-5, Big Ten 8-4, Big Ten Co-Champions
1926-27	Everett Dean	13-4, Big Ten 9-3
1927-28	Everett Dean	15-2, Big Ten 10-2, Big Ten Co-Champions
1928-29	Everett Dean	7-10, Big Ten 4-8
1929-30	Everett Dean	8-9, Big Ten 7-5
1930-31	Everett Dean	9-8, Big Ten 5-7
1931-32	Everett Dean	8-10, Big Ten 4-8
1932-33	Everett Dean	10-8, Big Ten 6-6
1933-34	Everett Dean	13-7, Big Ten 6-6
1934-35	Everett Dean	14-6, Big Ten 8-4
1935-36	Everett Dean	18-2, Big Ten 11-1, Big Ten Co-Champions
1936-37	Everett Dean	13-7, Big Ten 6-6
1937-38	Everett Dean	10-10, Big Ten 4-8
1938-39	Branch McCracken	17-3, Big Ten 9-3
1939-40	Branch McCracken	20-3, Big Ten 9-3, NCAA National Champions
1940-41	Branch McCracken	17-3, Big Ten 10-2
1941-42	Branch McCracken	15-6, Big Ten 10-5
1942-43	Branch McCracken	18-2, Big Ten 11-2
1943-44	Harry C. Good	7-15, Big Ten 2-10
1944-45	Harry C. Good	10-11, Big Ten 3-9
1945-46	Harry C. Good	18-3, Big Ten 9-3
1946-47	Branch McCracken	12-8, Big Ten 8-4
1947-48	Branch McCracken	8-12, Big Ten 3-9
1948-49	Branch McCracken	14-8, Big Ten 6-6
1949-50	Branch McCracken	17-5, Big Ten 7-5
1950-51	Branch McCracken	19-3, Big Ten 12-2
1951-52	Branch McCracken	16-6, Big Ten 9-5
1952-53	Branch McCracken	23-3, Big Ten 17-1, NCAA Champions, Big Ten Champions
1953-54	Branch McCracken	20-4, Big Ten 12-2, Big Ten Champions
1954-55	Branch McCracken	8-14, Big Ten 5-9
1955-56	Branch McCracken	13-9, Big Ten 6-8
1956-57	Branch McCracken	14-8, Big Ten 10-4, Big Ten Co-Champions
1957-58	Branch McCracken	13-11, Big Ten 10-4, Big Ten Champions
1958-59	Branch McCracken	11-11, Big Ten 7-7
1959-60	Branch McCracken	20-4, Big Ten 11-3
1960-61	Branch McCracken	15-9, Big Ten 8-6
1961-62	Branch McCracken	13-11, Big Ten 7-7
1962-63	Branch McCracken	13-11, Big Ten 9-5
1963-64	Branch McCracken	9-15, Big Ten 5-9
1964-65	Branch McCracken	19-5, Big Ten 9-5
1965-66	Lou Watson	8-16, Big Ten 4-10

Season	Coach	Record
1966-67	Lou Watson	18-8, Big Ten 10-4
1967-68	Lou Watson	10-14, Big Ten 4-10
1968-69	Lou Watson	9-15, Big Ten 4-10
1969-70	Jerry Oliver (acting)	7-17, Big Ten 3-11
1970-71	Lou Watson	17-7, Big Ten 9-5
1971-72	Bob Knight	17-8, Big Ten 9-5
1972-73	Bob Knight	22-6, Big Ten 11-3, Big Ten Champions
1973-74	Bob Knight	23-5, Big Ten 12-2, Big Ten Champions, CCA Champions
1974-75	Bob Knight	31-1, Big Ten 18-0, Big Ten Champions
1975-76	Bob Knight	32-0, Big Ten 18-0, Big Ten Champions, NCAA National Champions
1976-77	Bob Knight	16-11, Big Ten 11-7
1977-78	Bob Knight	21-8, Big Ten 12-6
1978-79	Bob Knight	22-12, Big Ten 10-8, NIT Champions
1979-80	Bob Knight	21-8, Big Ten 13-5, Big Ten Champions
1980-81	Bob Knight	26-9, Big Ten 14-4, Big Ten Champions, NCAA National Champions
1981-82	Bob Knight	19-10, Big Ten 12-6
1982-83	Bob Knight	24-6, Big Ten 13-5, Big Ten Champions
1983-84	Bob Knight	22-9, Big Ten 13-5
1984-85	Bob Knight	19-14, Big Ten 7-11
1985-86	Bob Knight	21-8, Big Ten 13-5
1986-87	Bob Knight	30-4, Big Ten 15-3, Big Ten Co-Champions, NCAA National Champions
1987-88	Bob Knight	19-10, Big Ten 11-7
1988-89	Bob Knight	27-8, Big Ten 15-3, Big Ten Champions
1989-90	Bob Knight	18-11, Big Ten 8-10
1990-91	Bob Knight	29-5, Big Ten 15-3, Big Ten Co-Champions
1991-92	Bob Knight	27-7, Big Ten 14-4, NCAA Final Four
1992-93	Bob Knight	31-4, Big Ten 17-1, Big Ten Champions, Preseason NIT Champions
1993-94	Bob Knight	21-9, Big Ten 12-6
1994-95	Bob Knight	19-12, Big Ten 11-7